Post-war British Thoroughbreds

A very fine example of a Triumph '1800' Roadster
excellently restored to original condition. Owned by
Mr. A. Harold, Chairman of the 'Triumph Roadster
Club', it continually wins the Concours d'Elegance
at the club's meetings.

Photo: Derrick E. Witty   © *George Rainbird Ltd., 1968*

Bruce A Hudson

Post-war British Thoroughbreds

Their Purchase and Restoration

All the illustrations in Part I are reproduced from the Author's watercolour drawings

Distributed in USA by
Motorbooks International
Publishers & Wholesalers Inc.
3501 Hennepin Avenue South
Minneapolis Minnesota 55408

FOULIS

Haynes Publishing Group
Sparkford Yeovil
Somerset BA22 7JJ

First published May 1972
Reprinted February 1973

Reprinted May 1976

© Bruce A Hudson 1972

ISBN 0 85429 136 9

Library of Congress Catalog Card No. 71–187270

Printed in England by
J H Haynes & Company Limited
Sparkford Yeovil
Somerset BA22 7JJ

Contents

Illustrations

Part I   Drawings and figures in the text

Part II   A photograph of each car described

Coloured Illustrations

Preface

In writing this book I was at first tempted to 'go it alone', only to find that working *in vacuo* is impossible with such a subject as thoroughbred cars. Whilst I have included within the scope of this book several of the more interesting mass-produced cars of the period, many of my thoroughbreds were individually built, so one cannot generalize or make sweeping statements about them. They remain individuals, and because they were hand-built, very often no two 'identical' models were, in fact, alike.

It is only the die-hard enthusiasts who, after years of experience with a certain model of thoroughbred, have any right to claim that they 'know' it. Therefore in many cases I have been glad to seek their very valuable first-hand knowledge.

I should like to acknowlege the kind advice and assistance given me by the following persons, some of whom have kindly provided excellent photographs for inclusion in Part II of the book. Without their aid I should have fallen sadly short of the degree of authenticity and accuracy that I originally aimed for in the historical and technical sections.

R.W. May (Allard)
R.A. Cox; D. Michie, Red Triangle Autoservices Ltd; O.N. Trent (Alvis)
A.M. Feather; K.L. Fuller; B. Joscelyne (Aston Martin)
B.C. Deacon, British-Leyland (Austin-Morris) Ltd.
I. Picton-Robinson (Austin-Healey)
D.J. Dyson, Champion Spark Plug Co. Ltd.
Public Affairs Staff, Ford Motor Co.
B. Hadfield; P. Skilleter; Mrs. M. Wheeler (Jaguar)
A. Davey; J.H. Lancaster (Lagonda)
A.J. Bagley; B.E. Smith (Lanchester)
C. Knapman; D. Purdy; L.E. Tyrell (Lea-Francis)
A.F.W. Rivers, Joseph Lucas Ltd.
B. Lacey-Malvern (MG)
P.H.G. Morgan, Morgan Motor Co. Ltd.
Peter Browning (Healey and Austin-Healey)
G.T. Cracknell; D.J. Morris (Riley)
C.G.D. Currie, The Rover Co. Ltd.
J.A. Enright; R.A. Fitsall; P.K. Rance; C. Sergison; T. Simpson (Triumph)
D.J. Elsbury; N. Hardey (Sunbeam and Sunbeam-Talbot)
Films and Photographic Department, British-Leyland (Austin-Morris) Ltd (Wolseley)

In collecting mechanical data concerning thoroughbreds it is virtually impossible to be 100% correct – 'standardization' often does not apply from one chassis to the next, even with the same model. Manufacturers' manuals and handbooks have, of course, proved a rich source for such facts, but due to the minute variations possible in specification, I am grateful to many of the above persons for supplying additional first-hand information and in many instances correcting my sometimes inaccurate 'gleanings'. Nevertheless I should like to make it clear that the accuracy of any material on a particular model is not automatically endorsed by *every* car club's Honorary Secretary whose name appears in the specialized sections. Also, whilst every care has been taken to supply accurate information throughout the book, its use and interpretation is entirely at the risk of the reader and no responsibility will be accepted by the author or his publishers for consequent loss or damage.

Certain publications too have been of great assistance: *British Motor Cars (1952)* by John Speed; *Modern Motor Engineering and Repair, Vol. IV (1956)* by Elliott A. Evans, which has proved a valuable cross-reference for the data pages; *Profiles* Nos. 4, 16, 60, 65 and 92; *Ford Facts* for details of Ford V-8 models; and *Healeys and Austin-Healeys (1970)* by Peter Browning and Les Needham, for detailed historical and technical information on these particular marques.

Finally I wish to acknowledge the unfailing encouragement given to me by my wife and parents and also several friends, among whom I should like to include Miles Marshall, of Foulis and Co. Ltd, who has ceaselessly advised and spurred me on through each stage of the original manuscript. It is this encouragement more than anything that has ensured the book's completion.

Newington, Kent   Bruce A Hudson
January, 1972

Second Preface

The popularity of this book on postwar 'classic' cars has made a second reprint necessary. It is gratifying to learn of how well it has been received by both Car Clubs and the private enthusiast alike.

I have received a number of letters since the book was first published, some complimentary, others citing points of detail where inaccuracy had unfortunately crept in. Compliments are always pleasant, but constructive criticism is equally as welcome; thanks to the ever-watchful eyes of Car Club historians most of these inaccuracies were put right in the first reprint. Now, in this present printing, further small corrections have been made.

Organizations for the preservation of the older thoroughbred car are apparently going from strength to strength. Despite economic difficulties, club members will never be persuaded to give up their main joy and ambition: to continue to run an often obsolete, but for them immortal, breed of car. The flag is being kept flying, and will ride the 'storm' all the more defiantly.

All of us 'old car' fanatics must see to it that British motor-cars of an earlier era are not allowed to suffer extinction, from whatever cause. Static museum exhibits, too, must be complemented by privately-owned models in which the 'spark of life' is kept truly alive in crankshafts that revolve and wheels that turn. What better display of sheer durability can there be than the daily appearance on our roads of forgotten, near-legendary marques, each example lovingly nurtured and restored, each living proof of inherent quality and its designer's vision?

Bacton, Suffolk
March, 1974

Bruce A Hudson

Part I

Purchase and Restoration

1 Choosing a Thoroughbred

Thoroughbreds the world over are beautiful creatures. But if you happen to be a car-lover, thoroughbred cars are the most beautiful of all. This is a book for car-lovers, about thoroughbred cars. However, before we start 'talking thoroughbred' in earnest we should be quite sure that we know what we mean by the expression. If we describe a stallion as thoroughbred we mean its breeding is impeccable. Its sire and dam, grand-sire and grand-dam, were of the very finest stock. This is fairly straightforward. But a thoroughbred car is more difficult to define. Indeed, by the end of this book, some readers will wonder why I have excluded certain cars and included others, and no doubt completely disagree with my choice.

Thoroughbreds, for me, mean cars that are precision built, cars that, at the same time — and this is where the disagreements will stem from — possess that strange magic that some call 'character', some 'style', and a few, 'breeding'. Although I have tried to stick to this definition fairly rigidly, 'style' and 'character' are such personal matters that I am sure that different readers will have different ideas on how well I have succeeded. Certain makes, with every right to be classified as thoroughbreds, have been deliberately omitted because of their rarity and, for quite a different reason, Rolls-Royce, Bentley and similar cars have been left out. This is because the book is for the majority of car lovers, not the privileged few who can dust down a gleaming Silver Wraith every Sunday morning. And just how 'privileged' are they? Some of the more modest thoroughbreds which this book deals with are just as much a delight to own.

The years immediately following the last war saw the production of some of the last of the classic cars. Although the outbreak of war brought car production to a sudden halt, the first years of peace heralded a whole range of fine designs, still bearing the stamp of pre-war individuality and style. But the cars of these great years, 1945—55, the last decade of 'the classics', were soon overwhelmed by the sudden flood of weak, passingly popular designs that were the result of the purely commercial response of manufacturers to a dramatically expanding mass market. The enormous demands of the modern market put an end to individuality of design and high-quality workmanship in most factories. The thoroughbred's day was over. The concept of the car as a utility article had arrived.

Be honest with yourself

But the cars of that important decade are still available to us today. Jowett Javelins, Riley 1½-and 2½-litres, stately Rover P3s and P4s, MG TCs and TDs with their unmistakeable pre-war air, the smooth lines of Sunbeam-Talbot 90s — the cars are still around if you are enough of a car-lover to go through the headaches of finding, acquiring, and running them. To *think* you are a car-lover is easy. The sentimental dreams of the great old cars swinging smoothly into the bends of some broad highway can be very misleading. The *idea* of being behind the wheel of one of those 'great old cars' is very different to the process of actually getting there. There is a world of difference between being a sentimentalist — a car-lover in the abstract — and a real come-what-may enthusiast. It is as well to decide quite honestly what you are. If you are a dreamer then the best thing for you is this year's mass-produced model. But if you are prepared to go through a lot of hard work and, not least of all, money, then you are the man for a thoroughbred.

Where to look

Although you must expect to pay out quite a lot of money on restoration and maintenance, if you choose widely your thoroughbred will not depreciate in value like most cars, in fact it will almost certainly *appreciate*. Many cars of the 1945—55 era will soon be collector's items; some of them already are. At the moment, the time is ripe for seeking out post-war classics. They are still sold quite cheaply and spares are still widely available which makes rebuilding and restoration a lot simpler. And the cars turn up in the most unexpected places — perhaps parked in an overgrown orchard gathering a front seat full of leaves or tucked away in Uncle George's garage behind his E-type Jaguar. You can often find them in a corner of a breaker's yard, left to themselves by a breaker who did not have the heart to add them to the pile of nondescript 'down and outs' littering the rest of his yard. Sometimes you see a brief glimpse of a shape that says 'thoroughbred' as it passes you in a village high street, and later see the same car outside a nearby cottage with a notice reading: 'for sale, £30 or near offer'. The cars are certainly there if you keep your eyes open.

How to choose

However enthusiastic you are, do not simply rush up to a thoroughbred seller and buy blindly. The first question to be settled before you even contemplate buying anything, is which car is for you. Of course the answer to this question is very much bound up with personal taste. You may be the man for angular, uncompromising lines like those of the Armstrong-Siddeley Hurricane, or you may prefer the smooth and graceful design of cars like the Riley or Jaguar. But there are certain factors which all prospective thoroughbred owners should think about independently of whims or aesthetic preferences.

First, the larger, and therefore the heavier, the car, the larger the engine required to power it. With the present steadily increasing fuel cost, a big car will mean prodigious fuel bills. Fortunately, many of the 1945-55 cars were equipped with moderately sized engines of about 1½ litres. In fact this capacity gives an excellent power-to-fuel consumption ratio. A conservative estimate of consumption for an average 1½ litre engine is 29—30 m p g; but up to 35 m p g is possible if the engine is in good order and the car is well driven on 'give and take' roads. The bigger engines, 4-5 litres and larger, can rarely manage better than 10 or 11 m p g. Another important point about your fuel bill applies equally to all post-war thoroughbreds. Their engines were designed to handle the post-war 'pool' petrol with an octane

rating of about 70. Today the 'regular' grade at 91 octane is quite good enough for these engines; in fact you may well see some sparkle. For occasional flashes of brilliance, use a 'mixture' grade at 95 octane. Generally speaking, the higher octane grades (97—101) are mere extravagance. You do not need to throw your money away on 'premium' fuel, and the way fuel prices are going up, the saving is substantial if you use 'regular' or even 'mixture'.

'Runner' versus 'Non-runner'

The second factor to be considered is the state of the car you are thinking of buying. Is it a 'runner'? If it has been used fairly regularly it is bound to be in better overall condition than one you spotted nestling in a corner of a breaker's yard. Even when a car is garaged or stored carefully in a warm cosy spot, deterioration inevitably sets in. Perhaps quite imperceptibly, time and disuse will be at work. Everything may look perfectly cocooned — the owner may have dusted the interior and polished the chrome every month — but under the bonnet and under the floorboards, the rot will have begun.

If you are confronted by a garaged 'non-runner' that interests you, it is not difficult to get an idea of its condition. Some things can be checked immediately. The battery is particularly vulnerable in storage. Its charge quickly leaks away, the plates become encrusted with sulphate so that they eventually disintegrate. All the other electrical components are particularly susceptible to the effects of damp. Tyres quickly become soft and tyre walls split. The exhaust system begins to rust and crumbles at a touch. The chrome begins to tarnish — despite the occasional polish — and the cellulose on the body starts to fade. But a lot more may be happening in less obvious places, places that you cannot see or get to easily. As piston rings drain of oil, corrosion sets in and they quickly rust to the walls of the cylinders. Brake cylinders seize up and crucial chassis members become rotten. A gearbox may gleam in the last rays of the October sun in some beautiful rural setting — but what no-one can see is that inside the gleaming alloy casing, two-thirds of the teeth on the second gear are missing. Without any question of doubt, a 'non-runner' is always a gamble.

The 'runner' is a great deal safer. A drive can show up its failings. A shattered gearbox will immediately chatter at you. An asthmatic engine will soon be gasping for that bit of power it no longer possesses. Faulty steering or poor brakes will quickly scare the pants off you. Old wives' tales about unscrupulous sellers putting sawdust in a worn gearbox to keep it quiet can be taken with a pinch of salt. A spell behind the wheel is always a very revealing test of a car.

The vital chassis

Nevertheless, bear in mind that there are a number of faults that cannot be detected by a short drive. Most important of these is the condition of the chassis. Most cars built in the 1945–55 era have a chassis frame of some kind, and a rotten and weakened chassis means the car is a danger to yourself and to others. In fact, the condition of the chassis is often the single most important factor when it comes to choosing a car. Repairs are very expensive — often prohibitively so — and definitely call for an expert, not a 'backyard welder'. Beware the owner who winds the car up to over ninety on the test run — he may be hoping that the exhilaration of the speed will make you overlook the condition of the chassis.

So, when you go to look over the car, take a pair of overalls, a sturdy screwdriver and an electric torch. Quite a lot of a car's skeleton is visible from underneath with the help of a torch. Take your time and look over every join of the chassis carefully. No matter how black your face gets, make sure you check each weld and those apparently inaccessible parts above the rear wheel arches. The screwdriver is an invaluable weapon. If you have any doubt about the solidity of any chassis member, jab it hard with the screwdriver. If it goes straight through you know the car is not

the one you are after. Do not be misled by a recently applied coat of underseal. This is an old dodge to cover up rusted parts of the chassis and adjoining bodywork. Fortunately, the screwdriver is unimpressed by appearances. A sharp jab always tells the truth however much of a cover-up job has been done.

Pipe-dream or reality?

A third factor for the prospective thoroughbred owner to consider demands a certain amount of self-criticism. How practical are you? How much time will you be prepared to devote to mechanical repairs and general restoration? Of course your enthusiasm for your car will boost your energies and determination, but it is as well to be frank with yourself before you start spending money. The job is going to take a lot of time and quite a bit of practical aptitude.

A fourth point is the amount of money you have available. If you buy the car for about £50 you must be prepared to spend four or five times this in restoring it to mint condition. Bear in mind though, that for a few hundred pounds you will have a reliable, attractive car that will actually appreciate in value as time passes. This is something few modern car owners can boast. Above all, you have a thoroughbred — a car with character and individuality, one that will give you endless hours of driving pleasure.

Always take your time

A final point is one of convenience. Does your house have a plot of spare ground, or will you have to park the car in the street outside your house? It is important — though not essential — to get the car off the road while you are working on it. The relative seclusion of your own drive or plot of land helps you to think clearly, something that is vital to systematic progress on the job. Working in the street leads to a feeling of hurry. Things get overlooked or bodged. And, although these problems can be overcome with a little self-control, you cannot avoid the fact that a street is a public place and you must not cause an obstruction or foul the pavement with grease and oil.

Many people who decide to buy and rebuild a thoroughbred keep their own, more modern car for daily use and treat the restoration as a fairly full-time hobby. It is a good approach because you always have a car to fall back on and any sense of urgency — which could lead to mistakes through rushing work that needs care and time — is completely absent. When restoration is complete, your modern car is very soon relegated to second place, perhaps it is simply 'handed down' to the wife, and the thoroughbred takes over.

Careful selection

Having said all this, we inevitably come back to the question of taste and personal preference. If you decide you *are* the man for a thoroughbred, you must think carefully about what it is you expect from your car. Keep your eyes open for thoroughbreds wherever you go and try to find out something about their various characteristics. Ask an owner why he runs a particular model. I guarantee his eyes will become strangely glazed and he will keep you talking for hours.

2 Decisions: The 'Runner'

So it runs — at least, the engine makes a noise and succeeds in moving the wheels! We mustn't be too cynical, but sometimes the dividing line between a 'runner' and a 'non-runner' can be a hair's breadth. So maybe we should assume that it is in 'reasonable order', *e.g.* the owner uses it every day and can produce an M O T certificate that points ahead into next year; or perhaps it is a second car the wife uses for shopping; or maybe the eldest son is learning to drive and takes it along the private road through the farm. Anyway, it is being offered for sale by a private agreement and not by a garage or salesman at some shady establishment. Avoid the latter types, the private sale is always the best. Garages and dealers are there to make as much profit as they can and are often experts in the subtle art of persuasion, so avoid them if possible.

Head not heart

First piece of advice — keep a level head. You may be overflowing with an inner enthusiasm to purchase — but keep calm. Over-enthusiasm (a common ailment with those who have a single passion or 'car-monomania') is often a wayward force that can lead you into a lot of bother and expense, and all for nothing. Something as small as a hair-line crack in the engine block or a decayed wheel-arch can condemn a car in the twinkling of an eye. You can't see it, you might never find it until too late — so what do you do?

Advertisements

Well, to begin — why is it for sale at all? There can be all sorts of reasons, some perfectly honest, some carefully concealed. But beware of taking the wording of an advertisement as gospel. Even the production of an M O T certificate doesn't in fact guarantee that the car will pass the M O T test next year. A great deal of deterioration and rusting can occur in twelve months. Perhaps the tester noticed the weakened chassis but 'let it go' just once more. Next time, that tester or another one may fail it hands down. So really the M O T only guarantees the satisfactory condition of brakes, steering and lights etc. at that particular instant. The very next day a major problem could suddenly develop in any one of the three systems, requiring large-scale repair work if it is ever to pass the M O T again. The line must be drawn somewhere — and perhaps it was drawn just before you came on the scene. The owner may have been warned by his garage that certain work would be needed next year before they'd let it pass again, and for that reason he has decided to sell 'while the going's good' and the M O T remains valid for an attractive number of months ahead. And remember that cars of the 1945—1955 era are getting a bit 'elderly'. No machine can go on for ever. Wear is bound to take place, but fortunately these cars were particularly well built compared to the workmanship and materials that are tolerated to-day. These cars were built to last — there were no murmurs of 'planned obsolescence' in those days.

It is the English climate more often than a car's owners that proves the worst enemy. High humidity and dampness take their toll. Steel, once exposed to air and moisture quickly rusts away and falls to pieces. And during the winter the widespread use of salt on icy roads means that each journey the car makes, a highly corrosive solution is sprayed with great force into direct contact with the metal parts of the underside. Over fifteen or twenty years, something is bound to take effect and you can't be sure that previous owners have been too bothered about prevention, let alone cure. Fortunately again the steel used in those days was of greater thickness than that used to-day. Workmanship and finish were of greater importance too, and because of this there was no thought of 'trading it in after a couple of years'. So there is a greater chance that the ravages of the English climate will have had much less effect.

Back to the beginning once more — that advertisement with its assurances of the car being M O T'd for several months ahead. Remember that the M O T does not cover merely the brakes, steering and lights. The chassis is just as important, and can mean 'kaput' next time round. So why is it for sale? The owner may be quite genuine about it — he's had it for quite a few years and has spent all the time and money he can on it, but the time has come for a modern 'family' car to take its place, and what with the wife and the new baby coming along, he is regretfully having to part with it. Or it may on the other hand be a young lad who 'picked it up for a song', has thrashed it around for a while, and then decided to 'pass it on'. You can usually tell, the moment he opens the front door. Most people are very poor actors.

Then the advert says 'engine in good order', and you have to decide whether this is true or not. After the chassis and its adjoining bodywork, the engine comes next without doubt. There is very little you can do once the thing packs up except put it right! Without an engine your pipe-dream soon tends to resemble a mass of dead metal, so this part of the car certainly is vital. But remember that a car with a sparkling engine and doomed chassis is worthless to you, whereas one with an engine in fair condition and sound chassis is quite another thing. You can always work steadily at putting the engine right over a number of years — the M O T test turns a completely blind eye to the engine, gearbox and transmission; but the crunch comes in paying an experienced welder to replace decayed chassis-members. This will definitely cost a lot of money, if it is done properly.

So let's assume you are going along to see the car, wearing some old clothes or carrying a pair of overalls. Don't be deceived by the owner's charming smile or his wife's offer of a cup of tea. Get straight down to the job and clamber underneath with your torch and screwdriver, looking for the 'catch' as regards that vital chassis. And take your time. Having made sure that things are sound 'down under', ask next to see the M O T certificate and log-book.

The best choice

By the way, by far the best model to choose when looking for a car to restore is one which has an alloy body and tubular-steel chassis, such as the author's 1952 Jowett Jupiter. This is the perfect combination that will resist the English climate for the longest time. An alloy body is much more resistant to the effects of atmospheric oxygen and moisture and cannot rust. Its decay comes eventually in the form of corrosion where the panels crumble away to a white powder (aluminium oxide) at certain spots, or where salt solution has attacked an exposed alloy surface and chemically eaten it away as aluminium chloride. But there is no doubt that an alloy body is the longest-lasting, and compared to a steel body, hardly corrodes at all. The tubular-steel chassis is made up from lengths of 14—16 SWG steel tubing welded together. This arrangement too is virtually indestructible, and should rusting and corrosion eventually occur it is quite a simple matter to weld in a new tubular section (of course, simple for an expert welder). But although the alloy-body/tubular-chassis is best, regrettably few cars of the 'glorious decade' had this actual arrangement, probably due to the high production costs (in 1952, the Jowett Jupiter was priced at £1500 — which made it quite an expensive car at that time). Most of these cars had a body of pressed steel and a chassis constructed from welded rolled steel channel or 14 SWG steel plate welded up into long hollow box-shaped beams. This latter type is much more susceptible to decay, and when it does, poses the problem of repair, in that large sections need to be cut out with an oxy-acetylene cutter and new sections welded in, where often there is very little actual metal left to weld to! The box-sectioned chassis has definite drawbacks but, if undersealed and maintained, can still be kept in perfect condition.

That log-book

So take a look at the log-book next. How many previous owners has it had? Just two — or is it ten? The fewer owners the better. One owner is the best — the car is obviously his 'passion' and not merely 'transport'. He will have polished and maintained it, nursed it, and tucked it up at night. Two or three owners doesn't necessarily prove anything. But above five or so, you need to start thinking, and remember, this may not be the original log-book. It may be log-book No. 2 — the car may have had twenty previous owners, and there isn't room to register twenty changes of ownership in one log-book. So look at the date-stamps and if the log-book looks quite new and the first date-stamp says '1961' then obviously this is not the original one. If it were, then it could be a very weary and scruffy-looking object by now. And if it is, then it should bear the date-stamp of the first registration *e.g.* '1948' for a 1948 model. So know what you're looking for when he hands you the log-book — a whole row of previous owners could mean a cumulation of troubles.

You should realise too that posession of the log-book doesn't necessarily indicate legal ownership of the vehicle. In fact it is no proof whatever, so be cautious to a degree.

Bodywork

Next, have a look at the condition of the bodywork, cellulose and chrome. No need to rush at things, take your time. Starting the engine can wait for a bit. Appearances can be deceptive, and in fact the outward appearance of the cellulose is not really very important at this stage. The glitter of the headlamps can be hypnotic — so keep a clear head. Re-cellulosing of the whole car, and even re-chroming of the metal decor are both completely feasible, given time and the necessary money. But when you go to look over the first 'thoroughbred', don't get things out of proportion. It's senseless paying too much attention to the 'flashy' aspect. What you should ascertain is whether the mechanical structure of the car is sound. Then, if it also glitters outwardly, so much the better! And even if it does look a bit 'tired', then at least you are sure that it's worth restoring and that you've got a sound basis on which to build. So have a look over the bodywork and take careful note. Pay particular attention to the places where a paint brush has been artfully whisked over rust patches in an attempt to conceal them. Here the rusting panel usually 'bubbles' up and is pretty difficult to hide. A little bit of rust is nothing to worry about; it can be cut back to the bare metal and re-built with fibreglass paste later. But large areas of rusting bodywork require a real decision.

Interior and engine compartment

Now have a look inside the car. Is it clean, 'tatty', or downright filthy? Most owners manage to wipe a sponge over the exterior paintwork, but often neglect the interior altogether. If it is spotless, then that is excellent; but if it's really mucky and unhygenic, time is going to be required putting things to rights, on top of all the mechanical and bodywork restoration. However, remember that there are good brands of upholstery paints suitable for P V C finishes or real leather, and that this same type of paint can be used to cover the wear and discoloration on door-panels. Also non-fray rubber-backed carpeting can be purchased quite reasonably and the head-lining can be strengthened and brightened by the application of a coat of non-drip tinted emulsion paint.

The condition and upkeep of the interior can be connected with the condition of what you can see under the bonnet, so ask the owner to raise the bonnet for you. Don't expect to be dazzled by what you see. It *is* possible — but only if one uses the car once or twice a year and spends the rest of the time mopping up and polishing! An engine, even in excellent condition, soon gathers dust and grime, so don't expect to see the sort of thing you find in machinery on display at the Science Museum. A very small seepage of oil from the engine acts like a magnet to road dust and soon builds up a layer of black grime, so if you find a rather dirty sight under the bonnet it is not necessarily a sign of neglect — the rotation of the fan behind the radiator sucks in huge volumes of dusty air each mile the car travels, and this dust has to stick somewhere. What you should look for are signs of real neglect such as oil oozing from the engine at the gasket joints, or dried splashes of rusty water on the sides of the bonnet interior. These are caused by the cooling system springing leaks, possibly revealed by anti-freeze when added in the winter. Look at the top of the battery and see whether it is covered in a layer of white powder and see whether the terminals are corroded. Open the radiator cap (*care* if the engine is hot! Better to leave this out!) and see if the radiator is full or emptyish. Ask where the dipstick is and pull it out. Is the oil up to the correct level or low? Or far too high? Could be a sign that oil-pressure is low and the owner hopes that an over-full sump will remedy it! Also look under the car for signs of oil drips. Look for frayed wiring. And a missing air-filter, for example — cars designed to run with air filters should not be run for any length of time without one. Is the fan belt frayed? Is everything rusty? When did the throttle linkage last see oil? Are the spark plugs rusted in? Has the near end of the exhaust pipe been patched up with a fire-resistant cement? If you've been underneath, you'll know about the condition of the rest of the exhaust system.

A very dirty engine probably has been neglected. But a 'dirty-looking' engine with clean battery, correct oil-level, good radiator, and signs of recent oiling of certain linkages could well indicate that it has been maintained — one problem being that the engine compartment may have been 'smartened up' for the sale, a natural thing for anyone to do. The paradox is that a filthy engine can be a sign of (a) utter neglect or (b) utter reliability over the years, necessitating very little need ever to open the bonnet at all. But the combination of dirty engine and dirty car interior can be generally taken as a sure sign of neglect. So bear in mind what you see — if the car is clean inside, then you can be much surer that the whole vehicle has been maintained, even if the engine does look a bit grubby.

Condition of the engine

After looking comes listening. Ask to hear the engine running. First point: if the owner starts it 'on the button' — fair enough. But if he mumbles something about, 'Battery's a bit flat . . . I'll have to start it on the handle . . . ' beware! There may be nothing wrong with the battery at all. What he wants to hide from you is the fact that the teeth of the ring gear (round the outside of the flywheel) are so battered by wear and tear that the starter-motor pinion fails to engage and merely grinds against the remains of the gear teeth (an unmistakable noise!) Replacement of the ring gear is fairly expensive, requiring removal of the engine from the chassis.

Once the engine is running, listen to it very carefully, with the bonnet open. Now, the present owner, although an enthusiast, may not actually be much of a mechanic. If there is a certain regular clicking noise from the top of the engine, this could mean that the tappets need correct adjustment; there could well be nothing wrong here except this. Does the engine tick over regularly, or is it 'lumpy'? Here again the owner may not have tuned the carburetter properly, and if there are two carburetters it is much more difficult to tune them together, anyway, so one must keep calm and not jump to too many evil conclusions. After all, a motor-car engine is a fairly complex piece of machinery and the owner may just be incapable of adjusting it accurately enough.

One should next listen for knocking sounds that come from inside the engine, indicating worn bearings (another expensive item to put right). But a knock could be coming from the dynamo, so place your hand on it and you'll feel it as the dynamo revolves. Do this also to check the water pump (may be hot!) and the distributor. Or maybe something is rubbing on something else; the fan-blades, for example. Not all strange noises are necessarily ominous.

But listen carefully for a deep regular knock or rumble. A long wooden stick or length of ½in. dowelling held against the cylinder-block or crankcase will transmit the knocking to your ear much more clearly and will help to locate it. The regular knocking sound could indicate big-end wear, particularly when the engine is idling. Ask the owner to rev the engine up, and see if the knocking disappears — if it does, then it is most probably a worn big-end bearing or bearings. You can check for this by pulling off one plug lead at a time — if the knocking disappears, then the worn bearing is in that particular cylinder. If on the other hand you hear a deep rumble at high revs, then the main crankshaft bearings could be badly worn. The rumble is in fact the crankshaft rattling about rather loosely against the worn bearings! Look for a bit of blue smoke from the exhaust, too. There could be quite a cloud of it if the pistons or oil-rings are worn, and you rev up the engine after a period of idling; this also indicates an 'elderly' engine with worn cylinders. But if there is a generally 'healthy' sound and no exhaust smoke, then all is fairly well — but do look for wisps of steam or dripping water (radiator or water-pump leakage or blockage).

Oil-pressure versus mileage

If the dashboard has an oil-pressure gauge, speed the engine up to medium revs and read the pressure. Anything from $40 - 70$ lb/in² is satisfactory, but lower readings could mean wear of some kind. Cold or heavy-grade oil can give a freak high oil-pressure reading; it's better to take the pressure after the engine is thoroughly warmed up. Generally for 1945–55 cars, an oil pressure reading at medium revs of anything below $20 - 30$ lb/in² is not a good sign, but the cause could simply be a worn oil-pump.

Look at the mileage meter. Remember that in twenty years the car has probably been 'round the clock' (*i.e.* 99,999+ miles) at least once, and it's almost definite that a complete engine overhaul or replacement engine has been necessary over the years (check engine no. with that in log-book or corresponding chassis no.). A glance at the clutch- and brake-pedal rubbers can give some idea of car usage, but these may not be originals either.

A test drive

The next thing, if possible, is for you to drive the car yourself. Make sure you are adequately insured; and perhaps 'take over' in a quiet road or lane. Remember that you are not used to the car at all, and each car has its oddities of operation to get best and smoothest perfomance. There is a certain amount of 'knack' with even the newest vehicle, and this one is certainly not new! The owner has probably offered to take you 'round the block' himself to show you how good the car is — or even along the nearby motorway at high speed. But that doesn't necessarily help you; however happy *he* is with it, it is your own opinion that matters most. Remember, he knows the car and how to handle it — you don't. And you're not buying a Rolls-Royce either — so give and take a little.

Checking the clutch

Firstly, the clutch. Sit in the driver's seat with the engine ticking over. Depress the clutch-pedal and engage first gear. How much travel is there in the pedal before the clutch disengages? If your foot has to be nearly down on the floorboards then the clutch is most probably on its last legs. Bear in mind that this particular model may quite probably not have a hydraulically-operated clutch, but it may be rod-operated by a direct mechanical linkage, so expect to apply more pressure than with the hydraulic system of a modern car. A 'spongy' feel in the pedal as pressure is applied tells you that the clutch is hydraulic, but that air has leaked into the system somehow, and will definitely need to be put right, or you're in for a lot of 'gear-crashing'. Let the pedal up again and notice the movement. There should be at least 1in. free movement after the clutch pedal returns *i.e.* the pedal should 'float' for 1in. before foot pressure begins to open the clutch plates. If you discover no free movement in the pedal, it could indicate a badly worn clutch where all the adjustment has been taken up to get the last ounce of wear out of the plates; or the owner in his ignorance has not allowed any 'float' on the pedal, causing unnecessary wear through slipping. How easy was it to get into first gear? Did you have to 'clip it' because the clutch wasn't disengaging properly? How about when you released the pressure on the clutch pedal gradually — did the engine pick up the drive smoothly, or did it 'snag' or jerk? All signs of bad clutch-plate wear; and replacing the clutch is certainly a long *or* expensive job — certainly not 'half an hour's work', but definitely no cause to reject the car outright (as in the case of chassis-rot). Clutch 'judder' also indicates the need for attention.

Gearbox and transmission

Now you're in first gear. Try rocking the steering-wheel and look for excessive free play. One inch free movement along the circumference is normal; a great deal of play definitely bad, and sign of wear in the steering-gear. Anyway, pull away carefully and try to get the feel of the clutch and gearbox, listening out for when you have to 'clip' the gear to get it in. Here again, you don't yet know the car, so make allowances for your own failings as well as the car's. A slipping clutch could be contaminated by oil getting on the plates. Difficulty in engaging the gears could mean a fault in either the gear selector or synchromesh mechanism (there is no synchromesh normally on 1st or reverse gears). Whine from the gearbox indicates general wear; a stiff gear lever probably means lack of lubrication, or in the case of column-mounted gear levers, the selector mechanism requires oiling or is out of adjustment. If the car keeps jumping out of gear suspect weak or broken selector springs. A simple cause of whine or stiffness is that the gearbox may be bone dry!

As a sales trick the owner could be using a very heavy grade of oil, such as 90 S A E Hypoid, in the gearbox to quieten it. But after a run, when the oil gets thinner, you should be able to detect a falling-off in smoothness of operation. Keep one ear open to vibration etc. from the transmission and a whining sound from the rear axle.

Brakes

Next come the brakes. Making sure it is safe to do so, slow up and apply the brakes with a steady pressure. Does the pedal feel firm, or 'spongy'? If it's the latter, there is air in the hydraulic system of the brakes. Does the car stop positively? Or do you have to pump the pedal up and down — another indication of air in the hydraulics. Or does it pull to one side? There may be a faulty brake cylinder on one of the front wheels or a worn, snatching brake-lining. Remember that the owner may not have adjusted the brakes regularly, and that could be the trouble, or lack of stopping-power could indicate oil on the linings. Squealing brakes can be caused by dust in the brake drums — but may be the rivets in contact with the drums because the linings are worn right down. As for the handbrake, it is linked indirectly with the rest of the braking system and if that is poor then the handbrake will be also. Very often the handbrake cable gets stretched in time, and this will render it inefficient.

Instruments

A glance at the instruments on the dashboard is also advisable during the run, notably the speedometer, oil-gauge and ammeter. Does the speedo work? And see whether the ammeter shows a charge at medium revs. Check that the ignition light goes out as the engine speeds up. If not, the generator or control-box need to be examined.

Final check, and price to pay

As you get out, just check the tyres, remembering that tyres do wear with use and cannot last for ever! In the author's experience the spare wheel is usually quite a pathetic sight — but regardless of its tyre (generally bald) do confirm that there is a spare wheel, even if minus its tyre. Without one, you can soon end up in a real fix, probably at the time of your first puncture. Without a fifth wheel you're absolutely stuck. And get a sound tyre fitted to it, not a balding museum piece.

Regarding the price you should pay, study the columns of *Motor Sport, Road and Track* and other motoring magazines and get some idea of the average market price that particular model is fetching. If the car has obvious failings, and you are prepared to take it on, despite these, then make sure you subtract a proportionate amount from the price the owner is asking to cover your estimated expenditure in putting them right. Or, if you arrive at a minus figure, and you still want the car, then still make some sort of allowance, and be prepared to haggle.

Well, that's about it. Perhaps this chapter may have given you the impression that every thoroughbred car for sale will have a million or so hidden faults — and of course that's not so. But forewarned is forearmed. Try not to look too suspicious of the whole affair or the owner will 'close up' and be on the defensive, often for no reason. Be friendly, but firm. Don't be governed solely by your head or your heart, but by a suitable compromise between the two.

3 More Decisions: Purchasing a 'Non-runner'

Compared to the 'runner', the 'non-runner' is a completely different kettle of fish. If you are going to take on a 'non-runner' you must be prepared to gamble a little and draw on your reserves of enthusiasm and determination to perhaps near their exhaustion-points. In fact limitless enthusiasm and vision are going to be essential — together with a deal of patience and tenacity. The advantages are several, the greatest being that you can pick up a 'non-runner' for virtually a couple of pounds (don't pay too much) and discover that your tinkering soon puts right what is mostly sheer neglect — one or perhaps two basic things being actually wrong mechanically, the rest of the vehicle needing little more than cleaning or polishing, or treatment against further corrosion.

Usually the 'non-runner' dictates the need for some spare ground or a place of some kind to park it that is off the road. Also you must not set yourself a definite time-limit as to when the car will be running reliably. It may take far more time than you originally estimated. But the sense of achievement in restoring a 'wreck' back into a 100% reliable and attractive car of very distinctive character is unparalleled and very worth the effort.

The breaker's attitude

The 'wreck in the breaker's yard' type of vehicle should be viewed with extreme caution. Once a vehicle arrives at the breaker's it usually never leaves; generally it is there for a reason or several reasons. Usually it has a condemned chassis, being the victim of severe rusting and decay. Or it could be a crashed vehicle, though this is rare for cars of 1945—1955; the vehicles themselves are rare and most breaker's yards are full of wrecked modern cars. But a car put aside by a breaker may be restorable, with a potentially sound chassis and body, if any corrosion present is caught early. The guidance offered in the previous chapter applies equally to the inspection of a vehicle that does not run, regarding the condition of the chassis and body, wheels and interior. But the owner of a breaker's yard is usually impatient, does not like wasting time, and is there to make money by whatever means he can. He will probably infer that you can 'take it or leave it' and will generally appear indifferent to your enthusiasms. To him, that rare vehicle represents perhaps a few extra pounds left as it is, rather than as breakage value, and he will hang on to it for a period of time, just in case he can find a buyer. But he won't fall over backwards for you.

Superficial inspection doesn't take too much time, but a deeper look at the engine, steering-gear, etc. at a breaker's yard will probably be awkward for you and you may jump to the wrong conclusions, either too optimistic or too

pessimistic, purely because there's no time to work it all out, particularly when he's breathing down your neck!

Private buying

The best type of 'non-runner' is one owned privately. The one, for example, standing in the orchard or nestling at the back of a derelict barn. Here you have all the time in the world, because as long as you can offer the owner the possibility of giving him more than £5 (the usual value of a complete car to a breaker), then he will let you tinker and clamber all over or under it for as long as you like. (Some breakers nowadays aren't prepared to offer anything at all for old cars but will simply remove them free and offer the owner nothing, so there's another trump card for you.) A good friend or relative may even want to give you the car, as long as you arrange a method of transporting it away.

As was stated before, the 'non-runner' is definitely something of a gamble. Without the engine running it is difficult to check adequately the operation of the clutch, gearbox, transmission and brakes. And the advice 'She was running when we stored her away' is not always very relevant after the passage of some years! Brakes, of course, can be checked if the car is towed, or perhaps pushed down a gentle slope, but with the engine running you can prove a lot more.

Tools, etc. to take

If you're going to tinker you'll need some tools. As a basic minimum a good strong screwdriver and a new adjustable spanner (with firm jaws) might suffice. But if you've a collection of BSF and AF spanners, take these along too. If you can, include a tin of 'Lusol' penetrating oil or 'Plus Gas', for those rusted nuts. And some clean rags will be useful. You may need a spare battery and a few other things (see below).

Chassis check

As with the 'runner', check the chassis first for soundness. This could be difficult, so try and jack the car up, putting wooden blocks (not bricks, which crack) to take the place of the jack before you get underneath. It is taking a very great risk to lie under a car that is raised merely by a jack; make sure that your chest and head are not close to any low part of the frame and that there is still space for your body underneath should by any chance the car slip off the blocks. Put wooden or brick 'chocks' on both sides of each wheel, apply the handbrake, and put the car in low gear.

Spare battery

The battery comes next. If it is still in the car, then in ninety-nine cases out of a hundred it will be flat, or ruined by prolonged storage in a discharged state, and may even be unchargeable because of deterioration. So the best thing is to come with a spare fully-charged battery (nearly always 12 volt type) of 50 amp-hour capacity, *i.e.* not too small. No engine will start with a flat battery, and even if the car has a starting-handle, a good battery is a much greater guarantee of success than trying to use one which is weak or in poor condition. If you 'borrow' one from another car, remember to stop experimenting before the battery gets too flat, or you may be unable to start the engine of that car when you put it back!

The owner may know

Before jumping into the driver's seat and pressing the starter-button, there are several vital points to check. Ask the owner why it was stored and whether it was due

to engine or other trouble. Having done all you can to ascertain any particular problems, and if there is no actual history of large-scale engine wear or worse (broken crankshaft, broken pistons or piston-rings, snapped connecting rods, and so on) it is well worth 'having a go' at getting the engine to run, since once it is running you can check the operation of the clutch, gearbox and transmission. But don't on any account waste time on starting a damaged engine. You may be successful — only to find that, for example, the first short burst of power snapped the other three con-rods as well! To be realistic, the engine in this case must be stripped down and put right first; and this job will be time- and energy-consuming and will cost money, so if the engine is seriously damaged, balance the pros against the cons before you spend any more time in tinkering. A broken crankshaft may cost in the region of £50 — £100 to replace including the cost of the new part and the charge for labour at a garage. If you want to do it yourself, in most cases you'll need a block and tackle to lift the engine out of the car; some engines with alloy crankcases (*e.g.* the Jowett 'Javelin' and 'Jupiter' engines) can be slid out of the frame, the weight-lifting requiring only two people. But motors with an iron block weigh far too much for this. So if you come across a wrecked engine, do think hard before you take the plunge.

4 Dirt and Determination: Overhauling a 'Non-runner'

In order to start the engine you'll need to obtain a fully-charged fairly large battery with terminal posts suited to the type of clamps fitted to the car's battery leads. Before doing anything else check the oil in the sump. If it is empty, or very low, you'll have to top up. If it's a cold day (and summer is the best time for tinkering with a senile engine) fill the radiator with boiling water to warm up the engine block. If the radiator leaks, or one or more of the core-plugs (metal discs pressed into the

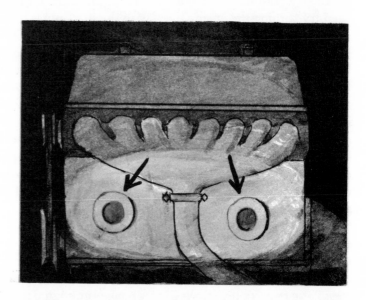

Fig 1 Typical position of core-plugs

water-jacket to fill the holes left during casting, see fig. 1) have blown out due to the cooling system freezing hard in winter, then leave out the radiator-filling altogether. A short burst of power of a minute or so 'from cold' won't cause over-heating or seizure. Filling the radiator, however, could be an instant check for a cracked block; water will pour or slowly seep from an invisible crack of this type and identify the fault quickly, more so once the engine warms up.

Necessary caution

Next, before you attempt to turn the engine over at all, remove all the spark plugs and pour a teaspoonful of engine oil, or preferably 'Lusol' or 'Redex', down each plug hole so that it trickles into the cylinders. The piston rings or oil rings may be rusted to the cylinder walls, and in this case the penetrating properties of the lubricants mentioned will free the rusted areas, if given a certain time to do so. Without this precaution it is quite possible to snap the rusted piston rings as you attempt to turn over the engine. Spark plugs that have rusted-in should be treated with 'Plus Gas' which should be allowed time to work. An alternative method for stubborn rusting is to apply 'Lusol' or 'Redex' liberally around the rusted thread and then apply heat from a blow lamp or burning rags soaked in meths or paraffin. The heat will cause expansion and the lubricant will trickle by capillary action into the threads, loosening the binding action of the rust. (The author realizes that the latter method sounds drastic and could seem dangerous, but he assumes that the carburetters and fuel-lines of the car will be bone-dry after many months of storage, and hence there should be no danger whatever of any petrol exploding. All inflammable items such as rubber-covered h t leads, etc. should be pulled to one side. The application of heat plus a lubricant is often the only way to loosen badly rusted parts. A light tap from a hammer via a sharp cold chisel can also prove very persuasive after the completion of the heat treatment!)

Allow a reasonable interval of time for the lubricant to seep into the cylinders and then try turning the engine over, with the spark plugs still removed, by means of the starting handle if fitted, or by pulling on the fan belt. Or you can put the car into a high gear and push it along. Whichever means you use, turn the engine over very slowly and gently at first. Should there be definite signs of resistance, think again before forcing the issue; the cylinders could be seized not by rust but by overheating many moons ago — this could, in fact, be the reason for sudden 'storage'. Anyway, better to leave the oil to soak in for a couple of hours rather than risk breaking an internal part. If you suspect rusted valves, remove the rocker-cover and inspect and lubricate as necessary. It is very rare for the crankshaft and connecting rods to jam solid through corrosion as their bearings are generally of white-metal, a non-rusting alloy; and anyway there is usually a small quantity of oil lingering in the sump, preventing corrosion.

Once the engine is free you can check the compression of individual cylinders, if a starting handle is fitted. You may find that there is very little compression at top-dead-centre in one or more of the cylinders, indicating severe wear of cylinders, broken rings, or burnt valves. So if you wish, replace the spark plugs and pull the engine over each t d c slowly. Later, once the engine is running you can verify your findings by pulling off each h t lead in turn and finding out cylinders with low compressions by noting which makes the least difference to the smoothness of the tick-over.

Getting her started

By now you should be ready to 'take a chance' at getting the engine to run. If you haven't yet done so, replace the spark plugs, connect the battery, and attempt to start from the driver's seat, unless the ring gear is badly worn, in which case use the starting handle. Switch on the ignition, look for the ignition light to come on, and listen for a rapid clicking sound that tells you that the car is fitted with an electric petrol-pump, (see fig. 2). The clicking should soon slow down and stop once the carburetter(s) are filled. Regarding the petrol in the tank (assuming that there is

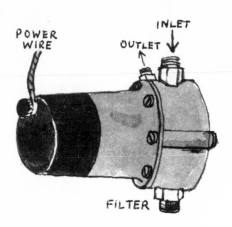

Fig 2 Electric petrol pump   Fig 3 Polythene "squeeze bottle"

any), if it is old it may be virtually useless for starting purposes. This point is often forgotten, most people assuming that 'petrol is petrol', however ancient. In fact, after a couple of months, the highly volatile fractions in the petrol evaporate, leaving the less volatile residue which is difficult to vaporize and makes starting virtually impossible 'from cold'. It may even contain rain-water or a lot of rust from the tank, and often it's better to drain the tank and re-fill with two or three gallons of fresh petrol of medium octane (95-97). Also, if this stale, dirty petrol gets into the petrol-pump it may block its filter or that on the carburetter, even perhaps filling the bowl with a petrol/water mixture. So check this too if you have suspicions.

If the clicking does not stop, but just carries on, switch off; you will have to investigate the petrol level in the tank (look for a reserve tap or switch) or try priming the petrol-pump to get it 'sucking'. Do this by unscrewing the petrol pipe joint at the carburetter and injecting fresh petrol down this pipe to the pump diaphragm using a polythene 'squeeze bottle' of the type sold in model shops as a container for model aeroplane fuel (see fig. 3). This action should fill the nearside chamber of the pump as well as some of the fuel pipe and get the pump working. Switch on the ignition for a short interval and look for petrol trickling from the pipe as the pump 'ticks'. Perseverance will succeed here! Once it's working, connect up the pipe to the carburetter(s) and switch on to fill the carburetter bowl(s). Sometimes electric pumps get stuck after prolonged storage, and if you know definitely that an electric pump is fitted to that particular model, but nothing is happening when you switch on, locate the pump itself (somewhere under the floorboards, to one side usually) and try slapping the casing sharply with your hand. This can quickly do the trick. You may have to locate blockages in the fuel line also.

If you switch on and the ignition light doesn't come on, check the bulb for deterioration or failure, and the switch and its connections.

No clicking at all may mean on the other hand that the car is fitted with a

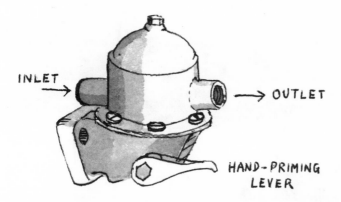

INLET

OUTLET

HAND-PRIMING
LEVER

Fig 4 Mechanical petrol pump

mechanical petrol-pump (see fig. 4), operated by the camshaft as it rotates. Go back to the bonnet and check this point. A mechanical pump, if fitted, is generally located low down on the crankcase. Try priming it as with the electric pump and then turn the engine over rapidly to draw up petrol; or look for a priming-lever under the pump body and pull it up and down until petrol fills the carburetter bowl having first made sure, by turning the engine, that the internal operating arm is not touching the cam lobe.

If you find that either of the two types is definitely faulty (more probable with the electric type) — there's no need to despair. You can still get the engine running for burst of a minute or so by unscrewing the carburetter bowl and filling it to just below the top with petrol by hand. While doing this, look for evidence of muck and rust blocking the carburetter jets, and clean them if necessary by removing them and blowing through each jet. But don't use a needle or other pointed object.

Once you've got the carburation side working, and ensured that the carburetter is in fact complete, that the plug leads are connected (in the correct order — most four cylinder engines fire 1-3-4-2 and six cylinder engines 1-5-3-6-2-4, viewed from the front) and that all seems satisfactory, press the starter-button. Don't worry if there's a leak in the radiator or if you couldn't fill the water jacket because of a blown-out core plug at this juncture — a couple of minutes' burst of power won't seize the engine; you'll only get trouble if you keep it running for too long and cause overheating. A frightening grinding noise from the starter motor coupled with failure to turn the engine indicates a rusted starter-pinion or worn ring gear.

If it starts and you can keep it running, let the engine warm up, so long as the cooling system is working satisfactorily for lengthy running. Then let it tick over and check the condition of the exhaust system and whether the ammeter shows a charging rate *i.e.* the needle is on the + side. Then try the horn and lights and indicators. If you blow a fuse, your trouble's not yet over! Should the radiator or water pump be faulty they will need to be remedied later, also. No charge on the ammeter could simply mean a broken fan belt or blown fuse; at worst an inoperative dynamo.

1951   AC '2-Litre'

1955   Alvis 'TC21/100'

1948   Armstrong-Siddeley 'Hurricane'

1953   Armstrong-Siddeley 'Sapphire'

1953 Aston Martin 'DB2'

1951 Austin A90 'Atlantic'

1954   Austin-Healey '100'

1949 Bristol '400'

1948 Daimler 'Straight Eight'

1950 Ford V-8 'Pilot'

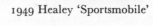

1949 Healey 'Sportsmobile'

1952   Jaguar 'Mk VII'

Ignition check

But what if you've tried all this, and obtained not a single 'cough' from the engine? Well, you'll have to check out the whole ignition circuit methodically. After several years, various ignition components may have broken down due to long storage in damp conditions, particularly the condenser and perhaps the coil; the insulation of the wiring may be decayed.

First remove a spark plug, reconnect it to its high tension lead, and rest the plug on the top of the engine so that its metal body is well earthed (see fig. 5). Being careful not to touch the plug, switch on the ignition and turn the engine over by hand using the starting handle (or the starter button, with an assistant to observe the plug). If you get a snappy, pale blue spark at certain regular intervals as the engine turns, then the ignition is working well. If the spark is quiet and a pink colour, then the high tension voltage is very low and probably the spark dies completely under

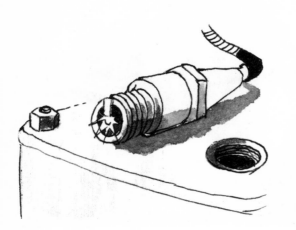

Fig 5 Checking the spark

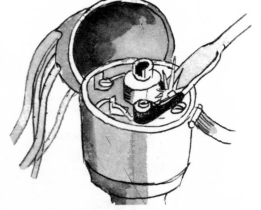

Fig 6 Charging the condenser

the compression of the cylinders; so in this case something in the ignition circuit is not performing adequately or perhaps traces of dampness are still present, leaking away a proportion of the high voltage before it reaches the plug (also substitute another plug in case the first is faulty). Long storage can also mean that the condenser needs 'charging up' — to do this remove the distributor cap (see fig. 6) and keep opening and closing the points with the tip of a screwdriver; gradually the sound of the sparks should become more 'snappy' and pale blue in colour as the condenser begins to charge and discharge correctly. On the other hand, a plug that is wet with petrol on removal is proof of (a) no spark or (b) faulty plug or high tension lead.

Ignition timing

If you've got a good spark, the trouble is carburetter or ignition timing. Bone-dry plugs probably point to stripping down the carburetter; a smell of petrol in the cylinders shows that the spark is coming in the wrong part of the firing-cycle, *i.e.* the ignition timing is out of phase. Check once again the order of the plug leads, then open the distributor cap and see whether the rotor-arm points to the contact that connects the high tension lead to that particular cylinder at top dead centre. T d c is found either by the direct method of introducing a piece of wooden dowelling into the cylinder through a plug hole so that it rests on the top of the piston, and is pushed up to its highest point when the piston reaches top dead centre (never use any metal object or it may jam and crack a valve, ring or piston) or by looking at the timing-marks on the flywheel which indicate t d c for No. 1 cylinder when they line up (fig. 7). Now find the clamp that locks the distributor in position (see fig. 8), loosen it, and turn the body of the distributor in the opposite direction to that in which the rotor turns. This advances the spark. Move the distributor only $\frac{1}{16}$ in. at first and re-clamp in position. Replace and reconnect all the plugs and try to start the engine again. Move the distributor by progressive degrees of $\frac{1}{16}$ in. until the engine

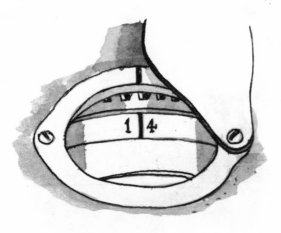

Fig 7 Timing-marks on flywheel

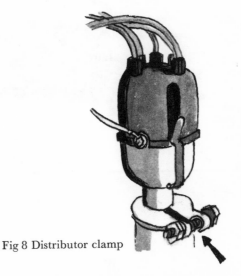

Fig 8 Distributor clamp

fires. A strong 'kick back' indicates the ignition has been advanced too far, so turn the distributor forward slightly. During this trial-and-error procedure remember to dry out the plugs occasionally if they get wet with petrol. Reference to chapter 5 and the data pages in Part 2 may also assist in accurate setting of the ignition timing.

Weak ignition

What to do if there is a spark, but it's weak and pinkish in colour? Check firstly for damp. If it's winter time, this is quite probably the case. In the height of the summer (the best time of year for 'tinkering') dampness in the electrics is improbable. Anyway, dry all the leads and connections, and the inside of the distributor cap. Leaving the bonnet open for an hour or so on a sunny day will usually do the trick and dispel tiny traces of moisture from inaccessible spots (except for the condenser, a sealed unit, which once penetrated by moisture rapidly deteriorates and is rendered

1955 Jensen '541'

1952 Jowett 'Javelin'

1949   Lagonda '2½-Litre'

1951 Lanchester 'Leda'

1951   Lea-Francis '2½-Litre Sports'

1949   MG 'TC'

1950   Morgan '4/4' Series I

1955 Riley 'RME'

1954   Rover P4-'75'

1953   Sunbeam 'Alpine'

1953   Triumph 'TR2'

1951 Wolseley '4/50'

useless). Check that the contact-breaker points are opening and closing as the rotor of the distributor turns. On a four-cylinder engine there are four 'high spots' on the cam which push open the points four times per complete revolution. Perhaps the clamp on the points has loosened and the gap between them is far too small, so check this, and re-set to 0.015in. with a feeler gauge (fig. 9). Also clean the surfaces of the points with fine carborundum paper — never sandpaper or coarse emery.

No spark — basic faults

But maybe you've drawn a complete blank — no trace of life at all in the ignition or faintest sign of a spark. This means you'll have to go back to the beginning and trace out faults methodically. The summarized procedure is as follows:

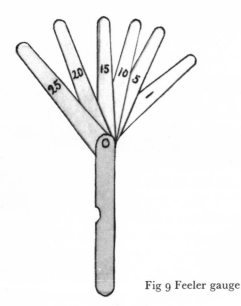

Fig 9 Feeler gauge

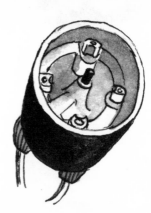

Fig 10 Carbon brush in distributor cap

1. Check battery for good charge, broken or loose battery leads and a good earth.
2. Check ignition switch is on, and all wires to coil and distributor are sound.
3. Verify h t voltage is being produced at the coil by removing the h t lead from the centre terminal of the distributor cover, and hold the end ¼in. from the metal of the engine block. Switch on the ignition and check that the distributor contacts are closed. Open and close the contacts with the tip of a screwdriver. Sparks should jump between the h t cable and engine block each time the contacts are opened. If not, check the coil and condenser for deterioration or failure by substituting replacements that are known to be operative.
Or 4. Points could be oxidized (clean with carborundum) or oily (strip out and clean whole assembly with a petrol-soaked cloth).
Or 5. Contact-breaker could be rusted to its pivot. Remove and clean (free rust with 'Plus-Gas') and re-oil with light machine oil (or '3-in-1').
Or 6. Adjust points to correct gap.
Or 7. Check that tiny carbon brush and spring are actually present in distributor cap (see fig. 10) and clean.

8. Finally check for fat blue spark with the plug removed, connected to h t lead, and rested on a metallic part of the engine while engine is turned over.

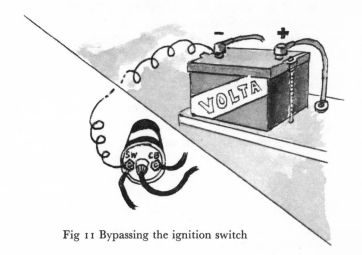

Fig 11 Bypassing the ignition switch

No ignition key

If you don't happen to have the ignition key (lost by the owner and no number engraved on ignition switch) the car can still be started by connecting a piece of flex between the unearthed battery terminal, (which was the negative on most cars of this period) and the SW terminal on the coil (see fig. 11). In the case of an obscure model, where the ignition key cannot be traced, you can get the car operative by either routing this wire to the dashboard and fitting a secret switch, or by substituting an ignition switch from another model (ex-breaker's yard) to which you do have the key. Door handles will also need re-fitting or adapting.

Priming the cylinders

It may be a frosty, cold day when you're trying to start that stubborn engine — you've got a healthy spark coming at the right time, but the carburetter seems frozen and the engine won't even splutter. Under such conditions, the petrol fails to vaporize sufficiently, and what with the fact that the engine has been 'lying dormant' for a very long time, you won't stand much chance of starting her. So a good tip is to purchase 4oz or so of Ether Solvent from a chemists'; this is a highly inflammable and very volatile liquid which will vaporize very rapidly no matter how low the temperature. Using a polythene 'squeeze bottle' fitted with a narrow spout (fig. 3), the engine can be primed with ether vapour, and the very low flashpoint of the ether will fire in the cylinders and get the engine firstly warmed up, and by continued priming, get a start. You'll need to remove the air-cleaner and then inject a small squirt of ether down the throat(s) of the carburetter(s) so that it vaporizes in the manifold. There is no danger whatever of wetting the plugs, since the ether rapidly evaporates, even from the interior of the engine, no matter how cold the weather. But don't go on priming the engine with ether if you fail to get a burst of power after three or four attempts — there must be some other factor that's wrong and preventing you starting; if it won't fire on ether, the ignition is definitely wrong —

you can discount the carburetter. Do make sure that you dry the plugs first if they are wet with petrol, before trying ether. And avoid any trace of naked flames or smouldering cigarettes when using it; its very high inflammability could cause a nasty explosion if you are careless. 'Quick start' aerosols could be used, but are not as satisfactory, as they contain upper-cylinder lubricant which will accumulate on the plug points after repeated use.

Engine noises, oil leaks

Let's hope that finally, despite trials and tribulations, you get that reluctant engine roused from its long hibernation and, albeit a little rough and bronchitic, revolving under its own power. If you hear popping from the manifold you may have a valve that's sticking; just leave the engine running and it should gradually begin to function correctly as the valve guide gets hot and expands. If there's a definite loud hissing, check the cylinder-head gasket, which could be partly 'blown' and is leaking gas from one or more cylinders. Revving up the engine will tell you about the condition of its moving parts: a rhythmic, multiple tapping is from the tappets, which are worn or out of adjustment; a knocking sound from inside the lower regions of the engine could be a big-end bearing gone; a deep rumble indicates main crankshaft bearings over-worn. Look, too, for severe oil leaks, and switch off at once. A glance at the oil-pressure gauge (if fitted) is advisable – if the needle stays around zero even upon revving, switch off at once also, or you may get a seizure due to lack of lubrication. Here, you'll need to check either the gauge or the oil-pump before continuing.

Seized clutch – remedy

The next thing is trying out the clutch and gearbox while the engine is running. But first you may need to inflate and repair punctures in the tyres. This done, you'll have to get the engine running again, then sit in the driving seat, push the clutch pedal right down, and engage first gear, (or any gear if you're unsure of the positions). Everything may go smoothly, and within a few seconds you're pulling away from a standstill for the first time. But more often than not, cars that have been stored where there are traces of damp tend to suffer from a rusted friction-plate inside the clutch, which virtually cements the clutch linings to the flywheel surface, rendering it impossible, no matter how hard one stamps on the clutch pedal, to get

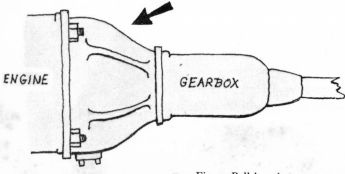

Fig 12 Bell-housing

Fig 13 Hydraulic reservoirs

them to separate and allow the clutch to slip as it should. The owner *should*, as a precaution, have placed a stout pole wedged against some low part of the interior of the car (*e.g.* the base of the seat) so that it held the pedal down and the clutch plates partly open. This way the clutch could not have rusted together. You'll have to jack the car up at the front (caution!) and examine the clutch assembly from underneath the car. Look for the bell-housing (see fig. 12), a large hollow casing immediately behind the engine, inside which the clutch rotates. Generally, at the base of the bell-housing, is an inspection cover of some kind. Unbolt it and you will see the hexagon-headed bolts that secure the clutch cover-plate to the flywheel. Turn the engine over slowly by hand, and partly loosen all these bolts. Having done so, insert a stout screwdriver under the edge of the cover-plate and hence apply leverage to the binding friction-plate which should now be clearly visible, thus breaking the cementing action of the rust and freeing it from the flywheel (due to the heavy springs behind the pressure-plate the friction-plate will still be held in close contact to the flywheel). When you've freed the friction-plate, re-tighten all the securing bolts *diagonally,* rotating the engine each time in order to do so, and marking the bolts with a touch of chalk to identify them. This procedure is usually successful. But on no account apply any sort of lubricant to the seized clutch — it will destroy the frictional qualities of the clutch-plate material.

Faulty hydraulic clutch

The unmistakable symptom of a clutch seized by rusting is the agonizing grinding sound as the operator tries to get into gear! It really is the most heart-rending mechanical noise imaginable! But perhaps the problem could lie in the hydraulic system, if the clutch is hydraulically operated. A quick way of verifying this is to look under the bonnet at the accessories clamped to the fire-wall — two hydraulic reservoirs (looking like small tin bottles — see fig. 13) indicate that both brakes and clutch are hydraulic, while one only will mean that a simple mechanical linkage works the clutch, this reservoir being merely for the brakes. If the clutch is hydraulic, and the clutch pedal has a 'spongy' feel as you press it down, then air bubbles have leaked into the hydraulic pipes and the system requires 'bleeding'. First top up the clutch reservoir, to where the shoulders begin to narrow, with the correct hydraulic fluid, either 'Lockheed' or 'Girling' according to the make of car. Then trace the clutch bleed-nipple and slip a two-foot length of transparent neoprene tubing over it. A clean jam jar should then be a quarter filled with hydraulic fluid, and the open end of the neoprene tubing held under the surface (see fig. 14). Get an assistant to sit in the car, loosen the clutch bleed-nipple, and ask your assistant to apply slow, regular strokes to the clutch pedal, while you get under the car and observe the air bubbles being pumped out of the system, and bubbling through the liquid in the jam jar. You'll need to top-up the reservoir pretty frequently so that it doesn't empty (start again!) For topping-up use only fresh fluid containing no air bubbles, however small. Your assistant should carry on pumping with slow, full strokes until you see that no more air bubbles are flowing from the neoprene tubing; then quickly tell him to hold the pedal firmly down while you re-tighten the bleed-nipple. If this is done correctly, the movement of the clutch pedal should now be firm and offer a definite 'solidish' resistance to foot pressure, without traces of 'sponginess'.

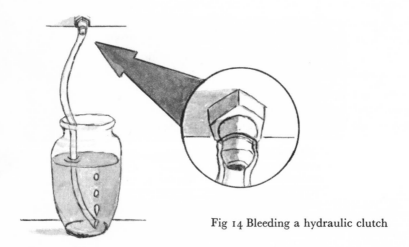

Fig 14 Bleeding a hydraulic clutch

Trying the gears

Once the engine is running and the clutch operating correctly, you can try out all the gears and test the steering and brakes by driving the car for a short distance (on private ground — there being no M O T certificate and hence no Road Fund Licence). Inability to select a certain gear could indicate a mechanical fault in the gearbox itself; almost definitely if the gear lever is mounted on the floor of the car and connects directly into the top of the gearbox. However, with a gear lever mounted on the steering-column the fault could lie in the rather complex mechanical linkage between the lever and the gearbox itself, it being out of adjustment, badly worn or in fact broken. Gearboxes are extremely complex in construction, too; a faulty gearbox is best entrusted to a specialist repairer, and to minimize the labour charge it's advisable to remove the gearbox from the car yourself and present it direct to the repairer. Some models allow removal of the gearbox from the car independently of the engine, while others dictate removal of the engine as well. But if you take the whole car along and leave a workshop to extract, repair and re-fit the gearbox, the bill will be quite high. Another approach is to purchase a second-hand gearbox from a breaker's and substitute it for the faulty one, *i.e.* 'take a chance'. Or, hand over the faulty gearbox and the one from the breaker's to a specialist and ask him to build up one good gearbox from the two, perhaps fitting some new parts, such as selector springs.

Brake types and problems

There are several possible types of brakes on cars of 1945—55 vintage: (a) fully hydraulic; (b) hydrastatic; (c) hydro-mechanical; and (d) fully mechanical. Fully hydraulic and hydrastatic are the most modern in concept (except for disc brakes), giving best stopping power, all wheels being fitted with brakes worked by hydraulic cylinders. Hydrastatic are also self-adjusting. Hydro-mechanical are older in design, being a mixture of hydraulic front and mechanically-operated brakes on the rear

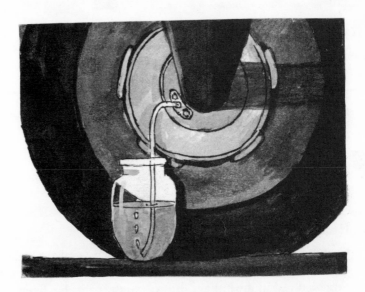

Fig 15 Bleeding
hydraulic brakes
on rear wheel

wheels (perhaps also intended as an anti-skid device). Fully mechanical brakes are self-explanatory. Fully hydraulic brakes lose their efficiency most when air bubbles have entered the pipes, and this necessitates 'bleeding' the entire hydraulic system as with a hydraulic clutch (p. 42) but in this case bleeding the cylinders of each wheel, starting with the wheel farthest from the master cylinder (see fig. 15). This will get rid of the 'spongy' feel at the brake pedal.

Hydro-mechanical brakes are not quite so easy to diagnose; the hydraulic section at the front may require 'bleeding', while the mechanical linkage at the rear may require adjustment to take up slack or wear on moving parts. Brake adjustment at the wheel is normally a matter of screwing in or out certain adjusting-screws or bolts fitted to the brake back-plate (see fig. 16). Turn each screw in the correct direction until the wheel just locks (jack it up and use hand pressure only) then unscrew the adjuster a couple of 'clicks' until the wheel is just free enough to spin. Do this on all four wheels. The front wheels may have two adjusting screws each while the rear will have one only, and this usually is square-headed, requiring a special spanner — or you can use a *good* adjustable spanner.

Fig 16 Brake adjustment screws on hub back-plate:

front wheel

rear wheel

Handbrake, re-lining brake shoes

Correcting the play in the brake-linings may also render the handbrake effective once more, or if it does not, the cable needs its slack taking up by means of a threaded rod in the linkage. But often the cable has been stretched beyond the limits of its adjustment, and here you'll have to fit a new one; it's best to keep the old cable as a pattern as often specialist workshops will make them up. Poor fully-mechanical brakes could mean bad wear in all the moving parts and linkages, but all three types will be poor if the brake-linings are worn out, and here the remedy is to renew them, obviously. You can sometimes save money if you can find out a cheaper substitute set of brake-shoes that fit the car, but are manufactured by a present-day firm that is still very much in business. For example, the rear brake-shoes fitted on the Jowett Javelin are identical with those fitted to the Series 1 Ford Consul Mk. I, and the Ford exchange price is much lower than that of shoes sold as 'Jowett Javelin brake-shoes'; and there must be hundreds of similar substitutes for most 'rare' makes.

Completely obsolete types can be re-lined by tracking-down brake-linings that are very near in dimensions to the ones required, and then 'juggling' with the rivet-holes to make them fit. No carelessness is implied in this; you need to make a good job of it, naturally. When rivetting, by the way, always start at the centre of the shoe and work outwards, ensuring that the rivets are holding firmly and that the linings do not have any 'spring' in them or tendency of lift off the shoes. Nowadays the trend is more and more for bonded linings, where the linings are fixed to the shoes with an adhesive, no rivets being necessary.

Hydraulic pipes should also be examined for leaks and hair-line cracks, and the rubbers in the master-cylinder may require replacement. The brake-fluid reservoir should be topped-up also, as with that for the clutch.

A tendency for the car to pull to one side upon applying the brakes shows that one of the front wheels is braking much harder than the other. This could be due to a corroded brake-cylinder rendered inoperative, oil on a brake-lining, a brake badly out of adjustment, a leaky hydraulic pipe, or severe binding due to loose anchorage of the brake shoes. A rhythmic squealing of the brakes as the car slows down and the wheels rotate slower and slower is probably caused by the drums having worn oval after many years of use. Squealing itself is usually caused by dust in the drums and is generally not harmful — just take off the brake-drums and wipe it out. Certain models necessitate a hub-puller for removal of the brake-drums, since the drum fits tightly on to a tapered shaft.

Steering and tyre wear

As for the steering, check for play at the steering-wheel first. One inch of circumferential play is permissible for the M O T test. Then jack up the front wheels in turn and try twisting the wheels independently, feeling for free play in the steering linkages. With old cars you can expect quite a lot of wear in these linkages, and often replacement is the only remedy. Regular greasing of the king-pins etc. minimizes wear. Sometimes there can be a method of taking up slack in the steering box, while thin shims can be purchased and used to take up play in worn parts that swivel.

Wear on the front tyres at the outside edges of the tread may be due to misalignment of the steering, and tracking should be checked for correct 'toe-in' (see Data pages) as soon as possible if you are going to get good service from your tyres. The garage that does your M O T can probably put this right for a nominal sum.

Transmission troubles

Certain models were fitted with a Layrub coupling connected into the transmission, its function being to 'iron-out' vibration by means of rubber brushes fitted between the gearbox drive-shaft and the transmission shaft. A worn Layrub will cause severe vibration at certain road speeds, and replacement is the only remedy here. Vibration problems in the transmission shaft warrant inspection of the Hardy-Spicer universal joints for wear, or a distorted shaft may be the cause. Sometimes the shaft is out of balance and this can be put right by means of a 'Jubilee' clip clamped round the shaft at a certain spot to correct the balance. This exact spot can only be found by trial-and-error (see fig. 17).

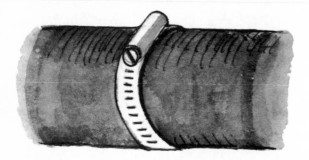

Fig 17 Balancing transmission shaft

If the clutch and gearbox are operative, but there is no drive to the rear wheels, this may be due to stripped gear pinions in the gearbox or to a sheared half-shaft in the rear axle. If the transmission shaft rotates, with no drive to the wheels, the trouble is almost certainly a sheared half-shaft or broken teeth in the crown-wheel of the rear axle.

Poor suspension

The car's suspension can only be adequately checked on a longer run. An uncomfortable ride comes from unlubricated or broken leaf-springs, faulty shock-absorbers, 'tired' torsion-bars, or loose or broken mountings for these parts. A 'bouncy' ride over rough roads indicates weak leaf- or coil-springs; but do remember that 'sports' suspension is much harder than 'saloon'. Faults are put right generally by replacement – often, for example, shock-absorbers are sealed units (see fig. 18). Certain types of shock-absorber need topping-up with the correct fluid, and can be overfilled. Knocks from the shock-absorbers can be caused by perished rubber bushes or loose mountings.

Fig 18 Sealed type of shock-absorber

Lights and instruments

Finally, check the lights and other electrical instruments for correct operation. A wiring diagram, obtainable through 'one-make' car clubs, is virtually essential for tracing any but the most obvious short-circuits. It is quite likely that a certain amount of corrosion will have affected many of the electrical connections during prolonged storage; an inoperative bulb, for example, may merely require the cleaning of its contacts with fine carborundum paper. There are usually a number of earthing-points throughout the car, and all these should be checked for corrosion. Faulty or decayed wiring can certainly prove a large headache. Only systematic checking-out of each section of the complex wiring-circuit will trace the faults; there is really no 'quick' way, and the process often requires infinite patience.

Have a go

As was stated at the beginning of the previous chapter, the 'non-runner' is much more of a gamble than a car that runs, and can require some months or even a couple of years of work to thoroughly restore. But very often it's the 'non-runner' that proves to be the rarer and more worthwhile model to the enthusiast.

So spare a thought for that poor old forgotten 'hero' you noticed last week, 'put out to graze' on a rough patch of land along the back road. Go back and take a closer look — and if you think you can supply the necessary 'surgery' and 'transplants' and offer the right kind of 'nursing home', dig down for your cheque-book and get working on plans that will eventually lead to a 'full recovery'.

5 A Much Closer Look: Re-building the Engine

If you're lucky, that engine may give you thousands of miles of service. But there's always the possibility that it's 'nearer the end of the road' than you'd imagined: lack of power, clouds of blue smoke, noisy operation, high petrol consumption.

If you're really keen on keeping the car and intend to use her as regular all-season transport, then a major overhaul is advisable sooner or later. A glittering exterior married to a bronchitic, elderly power-plant is an anachronism, and a virtual embarrassment. A thoroughbred should look well and run well.

Not worn, but out of tune

The normal symptoms of engine wear are high petrol and oil consumption, plus noisy operation and low power. But notice that these factors can be connected with 'apparent' engine wear; you could be mistaking incorrect maintenance and adjustments for what you think is actual wear. A maker's service manual is invaluable for correct adjustments, and although rather rare, a few manuals are still available for cars of 1945—1955, so you should do your utmost to get hold of one. The manual will give details of the correct tuning data for that particular engine — a lot of the engine trouble may be due to incorrect points-gap, spark-plug gaps, valve timing or carburetter settings. (At the end of the book tuning-data and other information is given for a selection of some of the more interesting thoroughbred cars.) So firstly, before you start dismantling, check over the setting of the ignition and the carburetter. Ignition timing marks often appear stamped on to the rim of the flywheel, and these markings may be observed through an aperture or by removing an inspection cover on top of the bell-housing (see fig. 7). When the timing marks are lined up, *i.e.* the appropriate groove in the flywheel rim and its corresponding groove in the casing coincide, the contact-breaker points in the distributor should just be opening. If this is not the case, loosen the distributor clamp or equivalent and rotate the distributor body either way until the fault is corrected. Some engines do not have marks on the flywheel but on the crankshaft belt pulley and the crankcase, see Data pages in Part 2.

If the contact-breaker points are badly burnt or pitted, renew them; also check the h t leads for faulty insulation, clean the plugs and re-set the gaps. Faults in the coil and condenser are best checked by the substitution of new units.

As for carburetter tuning, this is impossible on old and worn units, just as an elderly distributor with worn bushes and centrifugal advance mechanism cannot perform correctly at medium and high revs. To get the fullest benefit from an engine rebuild, fit new carburetter(s), distributor and spark-plugs. At least check the carburetter settings from the manual (or the back of this book) as regards jet and

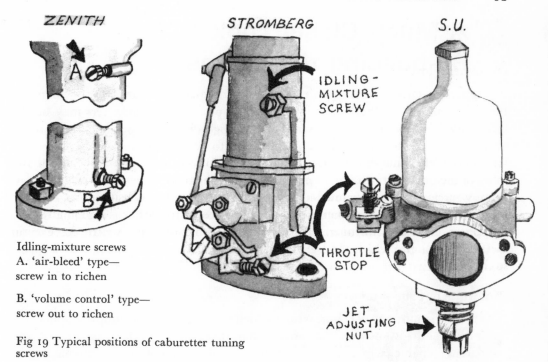

ZENITH

A

B

Idling-mixture screws
A. 'air-bleed' type—
screw in to richen

B. 'volume control' type—
screw out to richen

STROMBERG

IDLING-
MIXTURE
SCREW

THROTTLE
STOP

S.U.

JET
ADJUSTING
NUT

Fig 19 Typical positions of caburetter tuning
screws

needle sizes and compare them with those fitted to see if they co-incide*. Play in the
throttle spindle dictates the need for replacing the whole carburetter — you cannot
accurately tune the carburation if there's wear here. Correct tuning of the
idling-mixture is vital: set the throttle screw to medium tick-over, turn the
idling-screw until the engine reaches its fastest speed, then reduce the speed with the
throttle screw back to a satisfactory tick-over. Very small movements of either screw
have a considerable effect on carburation, and the adjustment of both screws must
be correlated. If two or more carburetters are fitted, they must be synchronized, and
all adjustments regarding tuning must be exactly the same on each, once they are
correctly synchronized. The most vital adjustment in synchronizing multiple-
carburetter installations is getting an exactly equal amount of opening on all the
throttles; without this, fine tuning is impossible. There is generally a rather complex
throttle-linkage on 'in line' multi-carburetter layouts, and identical throttle
openings are achieved by first accurately zeroing the settings of the linkage while all
throttles are held fully closed. This way the movements of each of the throttles will
be the same as they open up from the zero position. Tick-over is set in this case at the
maximum speed by careful experimentation with the idling-mixture screws of each
carburetter in turn; then the tick-over speed is brought down to reasonable rev/min
by means of adjustments to all of the throttle screws together. Any adjustment from
this point must be carried out in exactly the same way on each carburetter, *e.g.* to
richen the idling-mixture for better acceleration, turn each idle-screw by exactly the
same amount by noticing the angle that the slot in each screw moves through.

*See also jet sizes with modern fuels page 73

Throttles and mixture-strength both need to be synchronized; the engine should be well warmed up before tuning.

Oil burnt, or lost?

So apparent engine wear (with poor performance) may in fact be incorrect tuning-settings; and elderly distributors, spark-plugs and carburetters may be the main cause of this poor performance. As for high oil consumption, confusion can arise here also. After all, oil must be consumed to a certain degree in order to ensure long engine life. But what is a normal oil-consumption figure? A pint of oil per 500 miles or less must be considered poor for these comparitively slow-running engines. But is your engine losing so much oil by burning it, or by simply leaking? After a run, leave sheets of clean newspaper under the engine overnight and examine the oil droppings the next morning. Oil can escape from any joint where there is an inefficient gasket. Perhaps the main cause of high oil-consumption is loss by seepage, so check this first.

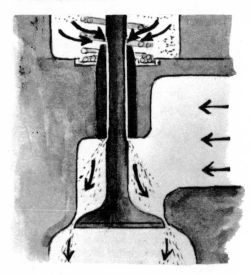

Fig 20 Oil mist drawn through worn valves and guides and into cylinders

Having done so, you still need proof that oil is being burnt. The colour of the exhaust fumes will show this quite simply. Take the car out for a run to get the engine hot, then leave it ticking-over for a couple of minutes. Now stamp on the throttle pedal to make the engine rev up sharply. Look back at the exhaust — clouds of blue smoke prove that somehow the engine is burning oil, *i.e.* in some way oil is getting into the combustion space and is burning with the petrol. But even this evidence is no reason for immediately stripping-out the engine, because oil can find its way down into the cylinders via worn inlet-valve guides due to the tremendous suction of the engine at high speeds (see fig. 20). To check this, all that needs to be done is to remove the cylinder head and examine the inlet-valves and ports. Evidence here of wet oil indicates the need for new valves and guides, the old guides being carefully tapped out using a soft drift of non-ferrous metal. In fitting new valves, the seatings need the merest trace of grinding to bed them in. This is a delicate operation, so use fine grinding paste, and only continue until you have a thin bright line all round the seating on each valve. Also ensure afterwards that all traces of grinding paste are removed from the port before re-assembly, and fit a new cylinder head gasket; the old one will not do.

After the above operation the car will need to be run until normal running temperature has been reached for a mile or so in order that all residual traces of oil are burnt away. Then repeat the 'sharp revs' test described above to see if the symptom has disappeared though routine checks of the dip-stick will soon produce irrefutable evidence.

Engine rebuild

But what if, after this, oil is still being burnt? Well, examination is required of the pistons, piston rings, cylinder bores, crankshaft and crankshaft bearings; a far more complex and time-consuming job than mere valve guide replacement. In fact, the engine will need to be removed from the chassis before work can commence on a major overhaul, and in the opinion of the author the best plan is to remove and strip the engine down to the 'short' stage, *i.e.* to the crankcase containing the crankshaft, connecting-rods and pistons only, and then to entrust the overhaul, replacement and re-assembly of this section of the engine to a reliable engine workshop. This way you will save a considerable sum in labour charges. The lazy 'drive it in and drive it out' method is expensive. You can always get a friend with a van or car with a large boot to deliver the 'short' engine to the workshop, and collect it afterwards. Engine removal from the chassis is not easy, but with an inexpensive block and tackle (see p. 176) and a strong overhead beam to take the weight, you can save pounds and pounds in cash. Also, work on the 'nerve centre' of the engine needs to be carried out with expert care, and if you're not quite sure what you're doing, incorrect and dirty re-assembly can wreck an engine in a mere few hundred miles. Since the tolerances in bearing and cylinder clearances are measured to within a few thousandths of an inch, 'guesswork' in this area is fatal.

So to be safe, entrust all major work to a reputable workshop or commercially-sponsored 'engine clinic'.

Wear tolerances

As a check, the following are the outside tolerances recommended for the moving parts of an engine; tolerances being the permissible excess clearance beyond the maker's recommended working clearance:

Crankshaft journals	+0.003 in.
Cylinder bores	+0.010 in.
Piston ring grooves	+0.006 in.
Gudgeon pins and holes	No vertical movement in boss No wear ridge on pin
Piston skirt	+0.002 in. on recommended clearance in unworn part of bore
Piston rings	+0.010 in. per inch of bore (use free ring in unworn part of bore, squared up at 90° to cylinder).

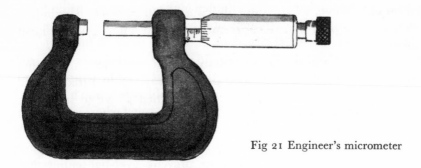

Fig 21 Engineer's micrometer

Clearances for piston rings, ring grooves and piston skirts should be measured with a feeler gauge, whereas crankshaft journals require a micrometer (see figs. 9 and 21). Comparison with the clearance data given in the maker's manual will also be necessary, but if this is not available the above table will serve as a satisfactory guide.

Nowadays manufacturers of pistons and piston rings offer special types for use in ageing engines with worn cylinder bores. By means of these, major top-overhauls may be delayed for thousands of miles. But it really depends on how much outside-tolerance wear you have; if in excess of the above limits you will definitely need new pistons, rings *and* a rebore of the cylinders — these special accessories cannot make up for excess wear. However, in some cases they may suffice; given below is a guide to the three stages of progressive engine overhaul:

1. Wear is in cylinders and rings only, but within above tolerances: fit special set of rings that limit oil-consumption.
2. Cylinder bores and crankshaft bearings within above tolerances, but existing pistons worn: fit special pistons to increase cylinder-seal and improve compression.
3. Cylinders, crankshaft and bearings badly worn: rebore cylinders (or fit new liners), fit new oversize pistons (or with new liners, new pistons to suit), grind crankshaft and fit new undersize main and big-end bearings.

A 100% overhaul includes the replacement of every moving part (except connecting rods and crankshaft) and every bearing surface with new; re-cutting the valve seats, grinding-in new valves and fitting new valve guides and valve springs. The camshaft and cams should be re-ground or polished and the rocker-gear and oil pump overhauled; a new timing-chain should also be installed.

Spotless re-assembly vital

It is possible to present the workshop of your choice with just the crankshaft and get them to grind the journals and supply new main and big-end bearings, or to present them with the block for reboring only. The risk here is that on re-assembly you may not be anywhere near careful enough regarding scrupulous cleanliness in the complete removal of all, *i.e.* every speck, of grinding dust from the crankshaft or boring swarf from every single 'nook and cranny' of the engine. This swarf can collect in the oil gallery of the cylinder block, invisibly adhering to the sticky oil sludge. Grinding dust, in a similar way, remains hidden in the oilways, *i.e.* drillings, of the crankshaft, and if either of these extremely abrasive materials is left inside the engine on rebuilding, extensive and costly damage will be done in the first few days of use. In fact the benefits of the costly rebuild will be immediately nullified. So none of this abrasive powder must be overlooked — all of it must be removed, and it is often here that the 'home assembler' falls short. A reliable workshop has a large dipping-tank containing a special solvent for this sole purpose, and whereas you may find it impossible to be certain you've been careful enough, their whole reputation and experience is behind their work. And re-assembly of the crankcase, big ends, etc. often necessitates a torque-wrench in order to prevent over-tightening and subsequent failure of certain vital high-tensile steel bolts; 'deep' engine work is definitely for the specialist expert.

But the 'short' engine stage is quite far enough for you to go and still economize very considerably on work bills. It is best for an expert to fit the crankshaft, connecting-rods, pistons and rings. You can also let him fit new valve guides and valves, etc. by taking the cylinder head along yourself. It's mostly labour that you pay for; materials are usually the smaller percentage of the total bill.

Finishing touches

And having rebuilt the engine, finish the job properly by thoroughly cleaning the exterior of the engine with 'Gunk' or some similar preparation, and re-polishing the crankcase (if alloy) or re-painting the engine block in the original colour with Hermetite 'Engine Lacquer'. Also fit new gaskets throughout, using the correct type of 'Hermetite' compound (red or green : red for alloy, green for iron joints), to ensure a tight joint sealed against leakage. Cylinder head gaskets require a thin smear of grease only. Pay careful attention to the fitting of the sump gasket, as this is usually one of the most likely places for oil seepage; and of course fill the sump with fresh oil and fit a new oil-filter element.

Running-in

Running-in should be done carefully. During the first 500 miles avoid letting the engine labour in any gear. Moderate revs will do no harm; but real harm is done by 'plonking along' in too high a gear. A re-fitted engine will be tight, and internal friction high at first, so allow for this initial stiffness and only indulge in short runs to begin with, avoiding speeds above 50 mile/h. After 500–1000 miles have been covered, drain the sump, re-fill with fresh oil (fitting a new oil-filter element to be doubly sure) and open out the engine to full performance speeds. A good 'workshop rebuild' may take longer than 1000 miles to completely run-in, but will prove the best in long term performance. Do not add molybdenum disulphide compounds to your oil, as these will only prolong the running-in period, and the same goes for a re-built gearbox.

Exhaust rebuild

A look at the exhaust system is advisable, too. Rebuild it if it's 'tatty' — a blown exhaust can cancel out all the good work you've done on the engine. On obscure

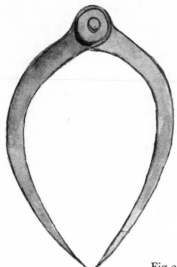

Fig 23 Rubber bushes fitted into exhaust mounting to absorb vibration

Fig 22 Simple type of external calipers

makes (such as Jowetts, for example — as the author knows to his cost!) find out the overall average outside diameter of the exhaust pipe using external calipers (see fig. 22), and then track down, from among the dark recesses of a friendly accessories shop, a modern silencer box with coinciding inlet- and outlet- pipe dimensions. By using a hacksaw, lengths of flexible exhaust piping (of coiled construction, employing galvanized steel with asbestos to seal the coils — obtainable from the more 'thorough' specialist spares shops), and a bit of ingenuity, you can soon work out a way of rebuilding the 'plumbing' so as to be satisfactory. Always assemble exhaust joints with 'Gun Gum' paste (or similar) to get an effective heat-proof and gas-tight seal, and install rubber bushes or grommets of some type in the mounting to allow room for slight movement of the system when the engine is 'rocking', for example, on tick-over (see fig. 23). U-clamps are obtainable, designed for exhaust assembly, but often a perfectly satisfactory joint can be made purely with 'Gun Gum' once it sets rock hard under the effect of heat, there being no need for a clamp. One technique the author has employed with effect is heating up the joint, not with the heat of the exhaust as recommended (where usually the wretched stuff blows out before it's set!) but externally with a blowlamp for short bursts or a small tin containing burning rags soaked in paraffin. This way you have definite control over the joint as it sets and can check that it's hard before you risk starting up the engine, also parts of the exhaust system can be assembled in the workshop this way beforehand. But welding is, of course, best and if you want to rebuild the exhaust by having it welded together, insist on a gas-weld as opposed to arc-welding; the latter results in pitting and hence weak spots, whereas gas-welding gives a beautifully smooth and thorough bond. Get all your bits and pieces together first and then present the welder with the lot — he may advise brazing if your assembly contains old, thin exhaust parts taken from the original system on the car.

Always try to get the length of the new exhaust the same as the original. Generally the length chosen by the designers is the best for that particular engine, as it is built to resonnate in harmony with the revs of the engine and also produce a scavenging effect to draw away exhaust gases from the manifold. So get the length right, and don't re-organize things, such as putting the silencer box right up at the front near the engine when the original design had it at the rear of the car. You may lose this vital scavenging effect and hence some of your performance. If you can, install the exhaust system high up off the ground and far away as possible from the spray from the wheels. In winter, this spray can be a strong salt solution and if it is not washed off with tap water can build up and eat through the exhaust within a few months. Also take care in 're-routing' not to bring the exhaust too close to flexible hydraulic pipes, the petrol line, or the fuel tank!

After a month's running to burn off any manufacturer's black enamel, give the entire exhaust system a coat of 'Kurust' and, when dry, a coat of 'Kingston' heatproof aluminium paint for prolonged protection.

After the first run

After the car's first run with a rebuilt engine, tighten all bolts, etc. that are situated at joints sealed by gaskets, while the engine is still hot. Use orthodox open-ended spanners and hand pressure — not the high leverage of a socket set. Seepage of oil from a hot engine can in this way be virtually eliminated; but don't expect to cut it out altogether — a certain amount is inevitable no matter how fussy you are. The cylinder head nuts in particular should be tightened well down while hot and in the correct order, as given in the manual.

Gearbox renovation

As stated previously, the gearbox is a complex piece of machinery and should be overhauled by a specialist. Since often the engine and gearbox have to be removed together, this is an opportune time to have the gearbox renovated. A good workshop is rarely reluctant to 'take on' even the most obscure gearbox, and for some reason is far more likely to 'have a go' with it than an unorthodox type of engine. Presumably gearboxes are much more similar in pattern. Automatic gearboxes (rare, however, on cars of 1945—55) are another thing, and if faulty can prove costly to put right.

To summarize, it's best to rebuild the engine, gearbox and clutch before you start on the bodywork; assuming, of course, the chassis is sound. This way you have a realistic and reliable vehicle that can be giving daily service during the whole of the period when you renovate the bodywork. Done the other way round, you could run into a double 'headache' and quickly lose heart in the whole project.

6 Outward and Inward Appearances: Renovating the Bodywork and Interior

The great enemy of steel bodywork is rust. Atmospheric pollution also attacks cellulose, and chromium-plated parts gradually tarnish under the action of an acidic or salty atmosphere. Even an alloy body is susceptible to corrosion, but at a much slower rate.

With the advent of fibreglass cloth and polyester pastes and resins, the thoroughbred car enthusiast stands a much better chance of replacing decayed bodywork successfully. But the job must be approached methodically and all traces of rust removed before rebuilding with resin. If this is not done, the rust will creep back under the repair and eventually sabotage all the good work. And rust is certainly a real bogy-man once it gets a grip! It's a real battle to eliminate it completely.

A face-lift

Some cars weather particularly well over the years. Your particular car may still be in excellent overall condition, more especially if the finish is still the original black cellulose, a very long-lasting 'colour'. In this case, rebuilding of any decayed areas need only be localized and sprayed-in where necessary. Usually blacks don't need matching up. Or perhaps the cellulose is good but discoloured on the surface or faded by prolonged exposure to sunlight. The remedy here is to apply a cellulose-cutting compound ('T-compound') over the cellulose, which will remove the top surface and expose the lower, fresh areas.

Bright parts

All chromed parts may be removed and re-chromed electrolytically at a plating works, but this is quite expensive. Very often, on removing chromed trims from along the sides of the bonnet or from the doors, etc., decayed and rusted bodywork comes to light underneath, Obviously this must be put right before replacing the re-plated parts. Headlamp reflectors are, of course, not chromium plated but coated with aluminium, so they should never be polished with chrome cleaner, merely a soft cloth. Certain specialists also will re-coat reflectors, at a price.

Dealing with rust

Probably you'll eventually want to re-cellulose the complete exterior, perhaps in another more tasteful colour, so here are one or two words of advice if you've never done it before. Firstly, those unsightly rusted areas. Here the rusting *must* be stopped *completely* before you attempt to rebuild, or the rust will creep back. To make the job easier, a portable electric drill with various types of sanding-disc and

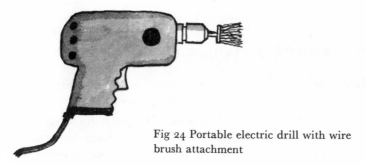

Fig 24 Portable electric drill with wire
brush attachment

wire-brush attachments is very useful (see fig. 24). All decayed metal should be
pulled away first by hand and then the rotary wire-brush applied firmly to the
working area until the rust is cut back to the bare metal. Doing this by hand with
emery-cloth, for example, is certainly going to be a long job, so an electrically-driven
wire-brush will definitely speed things up.

Once the rust is removed as completely as possible by mechanical means, a
chemical preparation is required to complete the job. Usually a weak acid, such as
phosphoric or acetic, is incorporated in most 'rust treatments', which dissolves the
remaining traces of rust and exposes the steel underneath. 'Jenolite' liquid is typical
of this type of preparation. Other types of 'rust-reatment', *e.g.* 'Kurust' take the
form of a paint which also contains a mild acid and is simply applied directly to the
cleaned steel surface. Yet others, for example 'Zinc Plate', are based upon
suspensions of zinc powder in a rubberized electrolytic paint, and like 'Kurust', are
simply painted on. The theory behind these types of rust cure is, presumably, that
zinc is highly resistant to corrosion. The real question is – do any of them work? In
the author's experience, the answer is: sometimes, yes; at other times, no. Each type
of preparation has it virtues; the problem being really more concerned with the
condition of the steel being treated. On some occasions rust-prevention can be 100%
successful, even when the work is somewhat slap-dash. At other times, after great
care with materials, the rust is found to creep through again after several months.

Several things are certain. Simply 'smarming' a rust-proof paint over areas of flaky
rust is useless, no matter what it may say on the tin. All loose flakes of rust must be
removed first. And you must do all you can to remove visible rust mechanically,
before entrusting anti-rust compounds to dissolve the remaining invisible rust
chemically. Secondly, each steel plate has two sides. You may be able to protect the
outside of a steel pressing against rust – but what about that inacessible,
unprotected inner side? This inner surface may be as rusty as the outside, and will
continue to rust away, if nothing is done to stop it. Rust seems to 'percolate' steel in
an inexplicable way. Before you realize it, it has crept, somehow, through the metal
and reappeared under the surface you treated, *i.e.* as long as one side of the steel
plate is still exposed to the corrosive action of the atmosphere, your 'preventive
treatment' is little short of futile in the long run.

So to guarantee success in your battle against rust, you must do something about
both sides of the bodywork you are treating. A messy, but very effective rust
combatant is either oil or grease, sprayed or painted on to the back surface of each

panel, *e.g.* if you're rebuilding the wings, treat the outer side of the panel with an anti-rust preparation and rebuild in fibreglass resin or paste, and then spray the inside of the wings with oil or paint the surface with grease. Bitumenized paint can also be very successful here, and though messy, provides good protection unless it is merely 'slapped over' uncleaned areas of flaky rust, where it is bound to prove useless. Bitumenized paint can be applied to clean, bare metal, but it is better to give the metal a coat of good quality black enamel first; also, once applied, no other type of paint can be applied over it, as its bitumen content is by nature non-hardening. Some garages offer 'steam cleaning and undersealing' of the chassis and underneath bodywork, and this could be one way of getting round a very messy job, as long as you are sure that they will do the job thoroughly. Or you can buy underseal and a strong wire brush and do it yourself.

Anti-rust treatment and primer application

Back to the initial stages of rust treatment. Once you've got rid of all visible rust by using, for instance, an electrically-powered wire brush, apply an anti-rust preparation such as 'Jenolite'. The manufacturers advise scrubbing it into the surface of the metal with a pad of iron wool, waiting 5—10 minutes and then wiping dry. After this, conventional paints, cellulose, or synthetic enamels can be applied. With cellulosing, of course, several coats of cellulose primer are necessary, but more important still are one or two coats of 'red oxide' anti-rust primer first, to seal the surface. After this has been allowed to dry thoroughly, it needs to be lightly rubbed down with fine 'wet-and-dry' abrasive paper (280A or 220C grades being most suitable for this particular operation) which is repeatedly dipped in soapy water as it begins to clog with the primer powder. Then several coats of grey cellulose primer are applied, allowed to dry thoroughly between coats, and likewise rubbed down using 280A or 240C 'wet-and-dry' abrasive paper for the smoother areas and 220D for the rougher. The 'brushing' grades of cellulose and cellulose primer can be applied by hand, and should be thinned with a 'brushing' thinners which retards drying-time slightly; or the primer may be sprayed on with a spray-gun (see below). Cellulose putty may be found useful for filling small indentations, but it must be allowed plenty of time to harden (2 — 3 hours) before rubbing down. The more coats of primer you have patience to apply, the better the resulting gloss of the final coloured top coats. After priming and rubbing down, the whole paint surface needs to be washed.

Differences in celluloses

Not all colours of cellulose are applied, or even dry, in the same way. Opaque tints, such as green and black, dry more slowly but do not need so many coats. Dark blue is an opaque colour, whereas pale blues are more transparent, needing more coats but drying slightly more quickly. Red, maroon, yellow and cream are fairly opaque, requiring less drying time between coats, but more coats need to be applied. As for white, this is the most transparent of all, demanding numerous thin coats, but least drying-time between them. Actual drying-times depend, of course, on the surrounding temperature, humidity and degree of ventilation.

Grey is a suitable colour undercoat for black, and perhaps suitable enough for white, cream and yellow. Red requires a pink undercoat. Maroon needs a pale-purple undercoat, and precautions must be taken so that no one area receives more coats than another, or the result will be patchy. White, yellow and cream need the same care as maroon to prevent patchiness. The application of the top coats of colour are described below.

Fibreglass, resins and pastes

But before we go on to spraying those vital final coats, we must deal with what must be done to areas of the bodywork that have completely rusted away and need rebuilding. In such cases, after anti-rust treatment has been carried out, it is best to apply a coat of liquid polyester resin to the areas of metal that are going to be bonded with fibreglass paste. This will seal the metal against contact with the atmosphere and will provide a good surface for resin-bonding or applications of fibreglass paste. Don't apply chromate primer here, or the fibreglass paste will bond merely to the coat of primer and not directly to the metal; eventually the primer may crack away from the metal, weakening the strength of the bond and allowing atmospheric corrosion to creep in once more. Manufacturers of fibreglass resins and pastes make quite an issue about providing a good 'key' for the resin or paste to bond to — a rough surface is best for a firm bond, so be sure to roughen the metal in the areas that are going to be in contact with the paste, and 'pepper' the surface with rows of drilled $\frac{1}{8}$ in. holes before you apply a coat of resin and then paste (see fig. 25). It is useless, by the way, to apply fibreglass paste over a gloss cellulose surface; here the bonding effect is virtually zero.

Fig 25 Rows of small holes drilled in panel as a key for polyester paste

All fibreglass resins and pastes consist of two separate components: (a) the inert polyester resin, in liquid or paste form, and (b) a chemical catalyst, usually some form of organic peroxide. Upon mixing the two, a chemical reaction takes place which also generates heat and the resin hardens. Without the catalyst the resin cannot harden at all; but once it is mixed into the resin or paste nothing can be done to stop it hardening, and in a relatively short time. Generally, very little of the catalyst is needed to harden the resin or paste. 'Fibreglass' itself is the name for a type of cloth woven from glass fibres, which, in conjunction with the resin or paste can be employed to build up a surface or form. In the case of glass-fibre laminating, layers of fibreglass cloth are bonded together with applications of resin; or fibreglass paste (generally a mixture of resin with an inert filler) can be used on its own for the same purpose. Resins and pastes harden more quickly when warmed; in cold conditions they take longer. One point to remember is that if the paste is to be applied in separate layers, then the heat produced by the chemical hardening of the first layers will speed up the hardening-time of subsequent layers, if applied after short intervals; hence a smaller proportion of catalyst needs to be added each time to slow down the hardening-time. If the same proportion is added each time, the hardening-time will get shorter and shorter and result in hardening taking place before it is convenient. Also, polyester resins and pastes harden throughout at an even rate, no matter how thickly they are applied, and irrespective of the presence of atmospheric oxygen. When set they can easily be machined, filed, ground, drilled, tapped and feather-edged. The paste, if made slightly thinner by the admixture of resin, or the resin if thickened with filler powder, can both be employed for casting or moulding, hence obsolete components or broken assemblies can be remoulded or repaired, often by injecting the resin *in situ*. Parts so rebuilt should not be expected to withstand extreme temperatures, *e.g.* on an exhaust manifold. To prevent surface adhesion to adjacent areas, vaseline or wax polish should be applied where appropriate.

Basic method

The basic steps for using fibreglass paste are:

1. Clean and roughen the working surface and treat, where necessary, against rust, *i.e.* use 'Jenolite' only.
2. Apply coat of resin+catalyst.
3. Mix catalyst with the paste in a general proportion of 30 parts paste to one part catalyst (or less,) and apply to working area with a knife or other suitable object, dipping the blade in Turps Substitute to help it slip.
4. After hardening, file or sand to correct contour.
5. Finish surface by cellulosing direct in the case of bodywork; primer is not essential.

Patching

Polyester resin together with glass-fibre cloth or matting may be used to patch corroded areas in wings or panels. After the necessary rust-treatment described above, a piece of glass-fibre cloth is cut to size, allowing about 2 in. overlap all round. After painting a layer of resin+catalyst all over the edges of the hole, the patch is then pressed firmly down to adhere well and well-saturated with more resin, using the brush. When this has dried, more layers of resin and cloth may be built up to the desired strength or thickness. Polyester paste may then be used to obtain a smooth finish by applying over the top.

Glass-fibre cloth or matting is not essential for use with resin and paste. Materials such as linen cloth or canvas, cardboard (as an initial support) or perforated zinc sheet are quite satisfactory.

Filling

To fill a hole in a metal surface, *e.g.* part of the bodywork, a patch is employed initially in order to provide a key for the subsequent layers of paste. The edges of the hole must first be lightly hammered inwards, thinner parts being actually folded over. Next the metal to be repaired is treated against rust. From the back of the repair, a glass-fibre cloth patch is cemented over the hole, using resin, and the cavity produced between the edges of the metal and the patch is subsequently filled with paste. Additional layers of paste are employed to build up the area until a fraction proud of the actual contour desired. Filing or planing then cuts back the hardened paste, ready for finishing. The patch could even be made using 2in. wide PVC sticky tape when filling small holes, and peeled off afterwards.

Shaping

Often the final shaping is best done with a 'Surform' type of rasp which employs a blade similar to a cheese grater. Solid wood-rasps and coarse files tend to clog up after a short while; but a coarse rasp may be used in conjunction with a long-handled wire brush for cleaning out the teeth of the rasp. Also you can begin to shape the paste before it is fully hardened. This method requires practice, but once mastered it can save a lot of extra effort and time. Use a 'Surform' rasp, with the paste only 'cheese hard'.

Mixing surface for polyester paste

For small work use the plastic tops from aerosol cans, *i.e.* the ones made of flexible plastic. When the residual paste is hard, flex the sides and it will drop out.

For larger work use a sheet of $^1/_{16}$ in. polythene or $^1/_8$ in. rubber about a foot square. To clean off hardened paste simply flex the sheet.

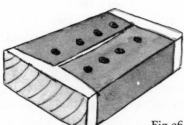

Fig 26 Abrasive paper tacked to wooden block for smoothing large flat areas

Large areas

Transparent plastic sheeting allows one both to observe and control the amount of paste applied while repairing large, flat areas of bodywork. In one method, the paste is pushed through the hole in the panel from the inside until it squeezes out against a sheet of clear cellophane laid across the outside. Before the paste patch has hardened, a sizeable length of flat wood of 1in.-square section is drawn rapidly across the cellophane with medium pressure, levelling the repair area to the general contour of the panel. After hardening, peel off the cellophane and finish the area with 'wet and dry' paper tacked to a block of wood, not merely held with the fingers as this can cause a rippled effect, (see fig. 26).

An alternative is to use a sizeable sheet of self-adhesive transparent plastic, stuck over the repair area, and to push the paste against this from the back of the repair. In this way the amount of paste that will be needed can be directly observed as you proceed. Of course this way of filling a flat panel must be done in one operation, sufficient paste having been pre-mixed. Carried out successfully, very little rubbing-down will be necessary, but do use the wooden block with the abrasive paper tacked on.

Non-ferrous packing

A good mechanical support for the paste is the metal used in pot-scourers of the non-rusting type; this is generally copper or brass wool. Ferrous metals, *e.g.* iron wool, should not be used as packing for corrosion will soon destroy them and weaken the repair. A hole in the bodywork can be packed with non-ferrous metal wool and the paste applied over this, where it is supported during setting by the fibrous metal. Perforated zinc sheet is also useful.

'Dropped' doors

Rebuilding a 'dropped' door is exacting work. If hurried or 'bodged', the door will be found still to close badly. Before rebuilding the decayed areas adjacent to the hinges, new hinges should, if possible, be purchased and fitted in the re-assembly. It is generally the lower hinges of the doors that wear out, or even come adrift, due to the bodywork rusting away. The hinges themselves are usually of non-ferrous alloy which cannot rust, but does wear fairly rapidly. Exposed, too, to all the salt spray from roads in midwinter, this alloy is quickly eaten away. The new hinges must be secured reasonably firmly to the strong areas of bodywork *above* the rusted parts first, say by means of $^1/_8$ in. steel strap, which can be readily purchased in foot lengths of approximately 1in. width, and often ready punched with ¼in. wide elongated holes. Quite a lot of 'juggling' will be necessary in order to find a way of doing this, and it is hence impossible to advise in a general way on a particular problem. What is essential is some type of reinforcement of the hinge supports using metal strap or plate, and brass nut-and-bolt construction. After this, the fibreglass paste applied in layers to build up the original contour has a sufficient 'key' round which to form a bond, while being reinforced by the steel. Whatever the manufacturer's claims, polyester resins are not a foolproof 'slap on' substitute for mild steel in this case. Where a certain amount of mechanical stress is present, a metal framework is essential as a foundation for the resin — attempting to somehow 'paste it all together' will *not* prove satisfactory. Using new hinges, the door should be packed up, so that it hangs well before the nuts and bolts of the support assembly are fully tightened. Perhaps merely closing the door may prove the best way in locating the final positions of the hinges. Fibreglass paste should be applied only when the door is held in a satisfactory position for a 'sweet' open-and-close action.

Securing bolts and screws

Fibreglass paste is also suitable for rebuilding a decayed spot that originally formed the location for a self-tapping screw. Here the screw is lightly oiled or smeared with Vaseline and the hole plugged with freshly-mixed paste, into which the screw (attached to its component) is pressed and held firmly. Upon setting, the paste automatically hardens to the exact thread-size of the screw and locates it firmly, the lubricant enabling unscrewing, if required. In the same way, bolts and nuts may be cemented into the bodywork, and after setting allow normal tightening and loosening (see fig. 27).

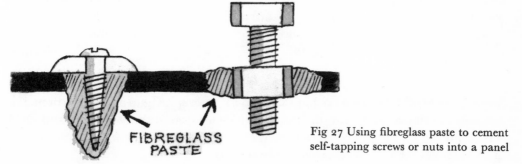

FIBREGLASS PASTE

Fig 27 Using fibreglass paste to cement self-tapping screws or nuts into a panel

Chassis must be welded

Fibreglass resins and pastes can prove an effective substitute for welding-in new panelling, etc. Of course, welding can be employed solely, without the use of fibreglass at all, and in the case of chassis renovation it is the only 100% effective and reliable repair method, particularly as regards long-term safety for the driver and his passengers. Pasting on pounds and pounds of fibreglass and trusting to luck, is sheer folly. A decayed chassis should be entrusted for repair to a specialist, and not a friend with a home arc-welding kit.

Bolt-on bodywork

On some models, wings, for example, are held in place by brass nuts and bolts, and here the best solution for a decayed wing is simply replacement by one in good second-hand condition from a spares specialist or breaker's yard. The colour will need to be matched with the rest of the bodywork by rubbing down the existing cellulose to a matt condition, priming with cellulose primer, undercoating, where necessary, with the correct colour of undercoat (see p. 60) and finally spraying-in with the correct colour of cellulose.

Re-finishing

All fibreglass surfaces need to be rubbed down smooth with fine 'wet-and-dry' paper before cellulosing, and any air holes and pitting should be filled and reshaped. Cellulose priming and undercoating is not vital, and unless there is some particular problem with the colour being applied, the cellulose gloss coat can be sprayed directly on to the washed fibreglass surface. Black, for example, being a very dense colour, does not necessarily need an undercoat, whereas red and maroon definitely do. Rubbing down an entire car's bodywork is a job for someone with patience and plenty of 'elbow grease' — so perhaps a sanding disc fitted to an electric drill is preferable, used correctly. The matching of old cellulose with new is always tricky — a lot of experimental blending of colour results rarely in a perfect match. Often it is easier to respray the whole car.

Re-painting

A complete respray can't be 'muddled through'. The right tool for the job is a compressor-driven spray-gun. If you don't own one you'll need to contact someone who owns and has experience in using one. Cheaper, aerosol-bottle-operated, portable spray-guns are not as satisfactory as the genuine article. As for aerosol cans of 'touch-in' cellulose, you'd need dozens for an average-size car, and anyway they would be hopeless for this type of job.

Preparation of bodywork

So first, contact someone who can loan you a proper spray-gun and who is prepared to help you respray the car; in the hands of a novice a good spray-gun can still yield very depressing results. Having secured the spraying equipment and a suitable clear space to do the job in, several factors need to be considered:
1. You should purchase sufficient cellulose or synthetic enamel and cellulose or synthetic thinners for the complete job.
2. All existing cellulose must be de-greased by rubbing well with Turps Substitute, and should be roughened to a matt condition, repriming if necessary. It is futile simply to spray the new colour straight on to the old glossy surface. Also the primer needs to be rubbed down between coats, and a coat or two of undercoat may need to be employed for certain colours (see p. 60).
3. All chromework needs to be masked with masking-tape and windows protected by newspaper taped into position.
4. If you're working outside, you must select the right day, preferably warm and dry weather, with no wind. This point is vital; cold, damp, windy weather is fatal — dampness in the atmosphere will cause a 'bloom' on the surface of the new cellulose, cold will retard drying and cause 'runs', and wind will cover the gloss surface with specks of dust. A warm spring or summer day is best, but don't work on a very hot day or in the direct heat of strong sunlight.

Spray-gun technique

The first coat of colour is a 'mist' coat, very thinly applied. The proportion of colour to thinning medium is 35:65 and most cars can be given this preparatory mist coat with a quart of the mixture, which should be allowed about a quarter-of-an-hour for drying. All the following coats will be of a thicker mixture of about 50:50 colour to thinners. With each successive coat the foundation will become firmer, so that the final few coats can be applied a little more richly by reducing the distance between nozzle and surface to be sprayed, and by dwelling a trifle longer on each section treated. The spray-gun is kept at a distance of at least a foot from the surface to be sprayed, which is covered by methodical long sweeps from left to right. When the spray is cut off momentarily, great care should be exercised when pressing the trigger again, or the spray will be of a very coarse consistency and may give a spattered effect.

Perhaps it is best to experiment in spraying a sheet of primed hardboard first, to get the feel of the job. Try to avoid an 'orange peel' effect, caused by spraying too close and for too long. Another danger is particles of semi-dry cellulose being deposited by accident on distant wet surfaces, where the particles are carried in the air — this is very easily done when spraying the tops of the window frames and the surplus spray falls on the roof panel, for example.

Five or six coats should suffice to give the required finish (see 'Differences in celluloses' page 59) but a good plan is to pause at the end of the third coat and give the surface a flatting treatment. This is a rub down with very fine 'wet-and-dry' (280A grade) and soapy water, followed by washing.

Spraying is an art and does require experience, so the beginner shouldn't try out his hand on any major spraying job until he has gained the necessary 'knack' by first attempting smaller jobs, where the results are not so vital. Small details, *e.g.* around the edges of chrome strips, etc. should be touched-in by hand with a small brush. The inside of doors can be finished by hand using 'brushing' cellulose.

Polishing

After the cellulose is thoroughly hardened, that is, after allowing a period of at least several days or even longer, the surface should be treated with cutting compound (a form of abrasive polish) which 'cuts' the surface gloss and prepares it for the application of a silicone-wax polish.

Synthetic enamels

Nowadays, synthetic enamels are replacing conventional cellulose, and these are applied in an identical way. Generally a completely different solvent is employed for thinning. They do not dry quite as rapidly as cellulose and hence give a slightly larger margin of time to the operator.

Outdoor difficulties

The spray-shop of an automotive engineer is generally fitted with blower heaters that maintain a steady drying temperature before and while spraying is in progress. It is kept free of draughts and dust. This set of conditions is the ideal for perfect results, and should be emulated as far as possible by the amateur; an outdoor spraying job can be seen to be a far-from-ideal setting for perfect results.

Preparations for renewing interior

A perfectly finished exterior should be complemented by the interior; retrimming the interior is quite a lengthy procedure. The car may be out of action for a while — say, in the case of the 'non-runner' where the interior is so decayed and unhygenic that the car is virtually unusable until it's put right. But in the case of the 'runner', restoration of the interior may be done in short stages so that use of the car is not lost at all.

Headlining

The headlining of an ageing saloon will probably be very faded or stained, definitely filthy, if not torn. Very often all that can be done is to replace it completely, and due to its filthy condition and situation near the roof, everything below must be covered before the work of stripping it out commences. So if you're going to adopt the 'short stages' approach it may be best to make the first stage concerned with renewing the headlining. Headlining material may be obtained through shops that specialize in car-trimming materials. As a rough guide, 3½ yds of 50in. material will be enough for even the largest cars; the washable type is slightly more expensive than the standard woven cloth. Stripping-out the old headlining should be done carefully because you will need it as a pattern for cutting the new material, so approach the job methodically, loosening the material above the windscreen first and working back towards the rear window. Having loosened the headlining at the front, you will see that it is attached further back not to the roof itself but instead tacked to wooden rails running across the roof. Be careful to use a tack-remover (fig. 28) and hence avoid ripping the tacking-strips, the dimensions of which you will need later.

Fig 28 Tack remover

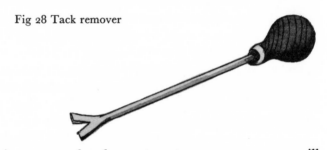

Covered in dust and the grime accumulated over twenty years or so, you will emerge with the complete headlining intact and, after unpicking the stitches, the pieces are laid over the new material as patterns. Obviously a sewing-machine will save a lot of time when it comes to making-up the new headlining. Copy exactly the dimensions and assembly methods used in the old one, incorporating the same number of tacking-strips and leaving the same margins of extra material.

Before you set about fitting the headlining into position, check the condition of the wiring to the interior light and that of the wooden tack-rails. Replace both if in poor condition, using mahogany treated with several coats of 'exterior grade' polyurethane varnish for the tack-rails. This treatment will damp-proof the wood. Again, use the old rails as your patterns.

When tacking-on the new headlining, start at the rear of the car and work forwards, tacking each tacking-strip to a wooden cross-beam. Do not stretch the material at all to tension it or you will run into fitting problems as the work proceeds. The sides are tacked last (see fig. 29). Finish by re-fitting the interior light.

Doors

Working downwards from the roof, *i.e.* keeping any dirt and grime always below your working area, the doors come next. The door panels must be removed and stripped of their old coverings (keep them for patterns, of course) and re-covered with leathercloth, using 'Dunlop S.708' as the adhesive. Sometimes it is just as well to dispense with pockets, etc. that were fitted originally – these will take much time and effort to reproduce. Panels originally attached to the doors by clips may be modified to employ self-tapping screws and cup washers, should the holes for the clips be corroded away. As for the panels themselves, should they require replacement due to decay or warping, ensure adequate waterproofing of the material you use. Very often rain water finds its way into the doors due to inadequate rubber seals around the windows. A choice of several panelling materials is possible: manufactured trimmers' panel-board, plywood, hardboard, Essex board or even rigid PVC sheet. The first is already impregnated against damp, whereas all the others except PVC will need to be treated. Coats of creosote or bitumenized paint will do, but apply plenty of whichever one you choose. PVC is unaffected by damp and hence cannot warp. Sheet of $\frac{1}{8}$ in. thickness should be used here, felt-backed to damp down the drumming tendency. In the author's opinion PVC is the best choice despite expense, particularly in the case of leaking windows – often a problem impossible to fully eradicate. Should windows still leak despite all efforts, then $\frac{1}{2}$ in. drain holes should be drilled in the underside of the door and several coats of bitumenized paint liberally applied on the inside of the door where any water might collect. It is this seepage of water that warps door panels and can soon ruin the appearance of a carefully restored door.

While the door is stripped out, examine the window-winding gear, door locks and catches, replace (if possible) all worn parts, and lubricate all mechanisms with a grease containing molybdenum disulphide. Then replace the rebuilt panel, all chrome strips, trims and door handles.

Interior panels

These are perfectly simple to restore. Remove them, strip off the old covering and re-cover with new leathercloth, using 'Dunlop S. 708' adhesive. Panels adjacent to the doors also retain the draught excluders and very often these will be 'bald' and need replacement; ask for 'Furflex' if your car was fitted with the furry type of draught excluders. New self-tapping screws and cup washers add that extra bit of smartness.

Seats

If you want to re-cover the seats it is best to remove them from the car; trying to do it with them still inside will be found virtually impossible. Most seats *can* be removed, the method soon being revealed by careful inspection of the fittings, and with them out of the car it gives you a better chance of inspecting and restoring the floor also. Seat covering materials range from the most expensive, hide *i.e.* real leather, through Bedford Cord to everyday leathercloth. Hide will be very expensive and if you make a mess of the job you will be sadly out of pocket. Bedford Cord is a woven cloth, very smart when new, but failing in that pale colours stain very easily. Ordinary leathercloth wears well but is not so comfortable and does not 'breathe', getting sticky in warm weather. Depending on your exchequer, the choice is yours.

After the seats have been carefully stripped, retain the old coverings as patterns.

Fig 29 'See-through' section of saloon showing method of attaching headlining to tack-rails, and construction of seat pleats

Interior seat structures can now be renovated; springs should be replaced and the frames painted. New hessian will give better protection to the spring interior. Unpick the stitches of the old coverings for patterns; pleated seats need a small extra allowance for each pleat, so examine the way the original pleats were made and cut the new material accordingly. You will notice that thin canvas is used under the covering in order to provide a 'pocket' under each pleat, filled with wadding (see fig. 29). So cut out another set of patterns in thin canvas, of idential size to those for the seat-covering, to be used to make new 'pockets' when you start to sew the covering together.

As with the headlining, a sewing-machine will make things easier. Even a hand-operated type will suffice, in fact may be better as its speed can be very carefully regulated. The new pleats are sewn first, the thin canvas being folded under the covering and the stitches placed at $^1/_8$ in. away from the fold. Use a strong thread, slightly lubricated with a vegetable oil to make it slip more easily, and a welting-foot attachment.

The original wadding may be used again when re-filling the pleats, or perhaps you may need to supplement it with some new wadding. A wooden foot rule is ideal for pushing the wadding into the pleats. Try to use full lengths and not odd pieces or you may get sags in the pleats after the seat has been in use for a while.

The skirt of the seat, *i.e.* the unfilled covering at the base, should next be sewn to the seat-covering, incorporating new piping if originally fitted. Examination of the original cover will reveal how this was done. To complete the work replace the new cover over the frame, tying it in place with new tapes.

Floor

Some thoroughbreds had a metal floor, others, plywood floorboards. In the first case, renovation may entail re-building with fibreglass as described earlier. Don't forget to treat all corroded areas against further rusting. A coat or two of black enamel or bitumenized paint will protect the metal against prolonged contact with damp. Remember too that, in semi-unit construction, the floor may be part of the car structure, so maintain it carefully.

With ½in. five-ply floorboards you can either replace with new, or protect the original wood with coats of polyurethane varnish or creosote.

Carpets

All carpet fasteners, *e.g.* 'lift-a-dot' types, where the central part of the attachment is fixed to the floorboards, should be examined and replaced as required. The old carpet is used as a pattern, the new carpet being cut from a rubber-backed 'non-fray' type of carpeting material, which does not require binding.

Harmonized interior

When planning an interior colour-scheme, often the exact matching of a colour in different materials is very difficult, if not impossible. A way round this is the use of specially formulated paints, suitable for application over hide or PVC (leathercloth) fabrics. Several firms manufacture such paints, matching exactly as regards colour, while differing in composition for hide or PVC. Hence a colour-scheme can be effected by the use of these paints, fabric seat-covers (*e.g.* stretch nylon) of a suitable colour being fitted over the seats, should it not be desired to paint the seats themselves. Also an elderly headlining can be brightened up firstly by vacuum-cleaning thoroughly and then applying several coats of (1) non-drip emulsion paint tinted to a suitable shade with artists' powder colour, or (2) artists' PVA colour, sold in large tubes. A coat of thick 'Polycell' may need to be applied beforehand to seal the material.

Small details

Wooden dashboards can be transformed by carefully sanding-off the old chipped varnish and refinishing with several coats of polyurethane varnish. Care should be exercised with walnut veneer, but solid mahogany dashboards present no problems. The inside of the scuttle or fire-wall should be rubbed down and given a coat of black enamel, where suitable. Also a vacuum-cleaner used behind the dashboard will probably remove dust that has collected there for far too long! All the chromed parts of instruments should next be polished — you may even be keen enough to remove the glass in the dials and clean the inside surface.

Hoods

Upholstery paints may also succeed in renovating a drab sports-car hood. Use the PVC type for hoods covered with synthetic PVC-coated canvas, and the Natural Leather type if the hood is covered in dirty, stained plain canvas. New hood windows should be cut from transparent 'Vybak' sheeting of 0.020in. thickness and stitched into position using strong carpet thread. Sealing the windows against water can be done with black Bostik 'C' — if you have a steady hand, and the necessary patience not to 'bodge' it! Black Bostik can readily be removed with paraffin, however. The author finds that 'Vybak' has a useful life of at least four years, used in all weathers including long periods of standing in warm sunshine, as long as it is not cleaned too often, and when it is, a very soft clean sponge and warm water containing a mild detergent are used. After four or so years, the surface tends to soften and lose its transparency; a remedy then is to varnish the windows with 'exterior-grade' polyurethane. This will definitely get you through the winter months satisfactorily, and will remain effective during that time as long as the hood isn't put up and down, where the flexing of the 'Vybak' will crack the varnish.

Sports car hoods can be rebuilt by a specialist coachbuilder, or you can do it yourself, noting the assembly method as you strip it down and using the old materials as patterns.

Wheels and tyres

As for the wheels — those of the disc type should be renovated in the same way as the bodywork, either spraying or painting by hand; spoked wheels may be refinished in silver cellulose. Tyres may also be brightened up with flexible black tyre paint.

All in all, the renovation of the exterior and interior is a lengthy job, but very worthwhile, as it both enhances and preserves the car and undoubtedly increases its value. Also you get to *know* your car intimately by this deliberate 'exploration' of its inner secrets. Generally speaking, the interior will also degenerate very rapidly if it isn't 'brought up to scratch' by an all-out effort sooner or later; no amount of dusting and vacuum-cleaning can eradicate that 'tired' look, once it has set in.

Part II
Some All-time Classics in Close-up

This section provides essential mechanical data for a selection of the most interesting thoroughbred cars of the 1945–55 era.

Due to the unavailability of maintenance manuals for certain (perhaps even quite a few) of these vehicles, such data should prove invaluable to the purchaser of a thoroughbred. It is, however, impossible to elaborate at any length on body and chassis construction methods, through lack of space, but renovation of these parts has been fully dealt with in previous chapters.

All the cars described are of British manufacture only, and have been selected by the author as his personal choice of those worthy of the name 'thoroughbred'.

The lists of data are, of course, no substitute for the vehicle's original workshop manual, but it is hoped that their concise, necessarily abbreviated content will prove 'a light in the darkness' to those confronted with a fascinating, but otherwise 'undocumented' marque.

All type numbers of carburetters, spark plugs, generators, etc. are the original ones as at the time of manufacture although the reader should note that the use of higher-octane-rating modern fuels may permit the substitution of smaller main- and compensating-jets to the benefit of both performance and economy. Lubricants also are those originally recommended, *i.e.* single viscosity 'straight' oils. Although many such parts now have modern equivalents, and multigrade oils have replaced the earlier types, it is hoped that the original specifications will prove of value to the thoroughbred owner, who may, for example, still prefer a traditional SAE 30 oil to something called 'SAE 20/50', and a 'Champion L10' plug to a 'quick-start, hot-tip, racing' plug made in Japan.

With regard to that most vital subject -spares- information is supplied, wherever possible, as to the names and addresses of specialists still able to offer spares for these rarer vehicles. Without doubt, membership of 'one-make' car clubs can be of great assistance and encouragement to the novice and a source of pleasure and good fellowship for the experienced devotee and so the addresses of the Honorary Secretaries of such clubs, where they exist, are also included.

Preceding the mechanical data are short histories of the development of the cars themselves; where possible, brief details regarding the design and fabric of the body and chassis have been added here, together with performance figures and individual features and failings. The descriptions of the models are also supplemented, in the majority of cases, by photographs.

The final pages are devoted to an Appendix listing additional sources in Great Britain of spares and materials, specialist services etc., which may prove of interest to the renovator.

AC '2-Litre'

1947-57. 2-litre Saloon.
4-5 seater

1951 AC '2-Litre'

The prototype AC engine of 1,991cc first appeared in 1919. Designed by John Weller, it was an ohc engine built mainly of alloy, with wet liners and cast-iron cylinder head. Total weight was a mere 350 lb. This first engine developed 40 bhp; by 1963 it developed 105 bhp, but basically the design was unchanged, having remained in production for forty-four years. The 1947 '2-Litre' Saloon, called the 'Greyhound', employed this well-tried powerplant in a chassis which had an underslung rear cross-member (the prewar chassis had employed a cross-member at the rear which itself passed above the shaft.) The engine was fed by three SU carburetters, the compression ratio was 6.75 to 1, and it produced 78 bhp at 4,200 rev/min, giving a top speed of 85 mile/h. In body design the 'Greyhound' employed streamlining throughout in a tasteful way, and yet the undue width of the boot, plus the low waistline and 'top-heavy' roof resulted in slightly ungainly proportions. Bodywork was of pressed steel. Brakes were fully hydraulic, but AC clung to the traditional leaf-springs front and rear as regards suspension. A floor-mounted gear lever was fitted, the gearbox itself having four speeds. A hypoid rear axle was employed and steering pattern was Bishop cam. The price, in 1950, was £982.

Features: Sturdy body on a rugged chassis frame. Thoroughly proven engine design; low engine weight makes removal easy. Fully hydraulic brakes.
Failings: Suspension, though satisfactory, rather unprogressive for a postwar design. Steel bodywork prone to corrosion. Three carburetters to replace, if worn.

	AC '2 Litre'	AC 'Ace'
Engine (Mechanical)		
No. of cylinders : capacity	6; 1,991 cc	6; 1,991 cc
Bore and stroke	65 x 100 mm	65 x 100 mm
Compression ratio	6·75 : 1	8 : 1
Valve layout	Overhead (ohc)	Overhead (ohc)
Tappet clearances	0·020 in. (hot)	0·020 in. (hot)
Location of valve timing marks	On flywheel	On flywheel
Timing : inlet valve opens	12° btdc	12° btdc
Piston withdrawal direction	Wet liners removed with pistons	
Engine (Ignition)		
Firing order	1, 5, 3, 6, 2, 4	1, 5, 3, 6, 2, 4
Location of timing marks	—	—
Timing : points open	20° btdc (1 — 6)	20° btdc (1 — 6)
Original spark plugs	Lodge HN	Lodge HN
Plug gap	0·015—0·018 in.	0·015—0·018 in.
Original (Lucas) coil	Q 12	HS 12
Original (Lucas) distributor	DX6A	DM6
Carburetters		
Original make	3 SU	3 SU
Original type	H 4	H 4
Metering needle	DW	DW
Electrical Accessories		
Battery	12v 60 ah	12v 60 ah
Original (Lucas) generator	C45PV/3	C39PV/2
Original (Lucas) control box	RF96/2	RB106/1
Original (Lucas) starter motor	M418G	M418G
Chassis Components and Steering Geometry		
Brakes	Girling hydraulic	Girling hydraulic
Rear axle : Type	Hypoid bevel	Hypoid bevel
Ratio	4·55 : 1	3·64 : 1
Crown-wheel tooth contact	(No adjustment details)	—
Front suspension	Semi-elliptic leaf	Transverse leaf and wishbones
Rear suspension	Semi-elliptic leaf	Independent transverse leaf
Steering Pattern	Bishop cam	Bishop cam
Toe-in	$^3/_{16}$ in.	$^1/_{16}$ in.
Castor angle	2½ — 3°	5°
Camber angle	2½°	1 — 2°
King-pin inclination	7½°	9°
Lubrication		
Engine : Original S.A.E. grade	Summer 40, Winter 30	Summer 40, Winter 30
Quantity	14 pt.	14 pt.
Gearbox : Original S.A.E. grade	Summer 40, Winter 30	Summer 40, Winter 30
Quantity	3 pt.	3 pt.
Rear axle : Original S.A.E. grade	90 HYP	90 HYP
Quantity	3 pt.	3½ pt.
Steering box : Original S.A.E. grade	90 EP	90 EP
Tyres		
Size	6·70 x 16	5·50 x 16
Pressures (lb/in^2)	F : 22 R : 22	F : 22 R : 24

AC 'Ace'

1953-56. 2-litre Sports. 2 seater

Based on a design by John Tojeiro, the first 'Ace' two-seater employed the traditional AC engine of 1,991cc, with compression ratio raised to 8 to 1, and with carburation supplied by three SUs. By 1955 this unit developed 90 bhp at 4,500 rev/min, top speed then being 103 mile/h. The chassis was of welded steel tubes and the bodywork of aluminium; unladen weight was a mere 16½ cwt. The body design was very clean and modern with fully cowled engine and a low oval radiator grille. The headlamps were fully blended into the front wings, the line of both wings being smooth and undulating while still leaving the wheels fully exposed. Wire wheels were fitted as standard equipment, and access to the cockpit was by small, very neat doors. The whole outward design, in fact, was reminiscent of the prototype Jowett Jupiter R4 of 1951 (which never reached production) and also resembled the Austin-Healey '100' of 1953, the performance of which was very similar. Suspension was independent on all four wheels, yet incorporating the die-hard principle of using leaf-springs throughout. Fully hydraulic brakes were fitted, together with a hypoid final drive with De Dion axle, Bishop cam steering, and floor-mounted gear lever to a four-speed gearbox. Road holding qualities were excellent, and far superior to its mass-produced 2-litre rivals of the time.

Features: High performance; clean, un-dated, compact design. Aluminium body plus tubular steel chassis, the ideal combination for complete restoration and preservation. Fully hydraulic brakes. Alloy engine very light in weight and easy to handle if rebuilding.

Failings: Three carburetters pose difficulties in tuning and high cost of replacement, if worn. Alloy engine may suffer from internal corrosion; steel studs require care — overtightening can strip the alloy threads; alloy castings distort easily.

Car Club Honorary Secretary: '**Lynton**', 1 North **Drive**, Ruislip, Middx.

SPARES: 1. Through AC Cars, Ltd., Thames Ditton (to a degree.)
           2. Through the above club.

1954 AC 'Ace' prototype

Allard 'M2X'

1950-53. 3½-litre Drophead Coupe. 4 seater

An enthusiastic racing driver in both prewar and postwar events, Sidney Allard formed his own car company in 1936. Ford components were employed in the main, in the way that Donald Healey used first Riley and then Austin engines and mechanical parts. Full production commenced in 1946 with the 'L', and later 'K1', 'K2' and 'M' models, all of these being powered by a Ford V-8 'Pilot' engine of eight-cylinder side-valve 'V' pattern, 3,622cc capacity and 6.15 to 1 compression ratio, developing 85 bhp at 3,500 rev/min. The large 'inverted T'-shaped grille of the 1950 model gave way later to an abbreviated design which in overall outline was reminiscent of a capital 'A'; apart from a new one-piece bumper, the front of the car remained little changed. The rear of the car differed in that the rear wheels were half enclosed within wings that were merely a continuation of the integral form of the bonnet and doors. The 'M2X' was fitted with the Allard divided front axle, front suspension being by independent coil springs. The rear axle was of the spiral bevel type, rear suspension being of transverse leaf-spring pattern. A Ford three-speed gearbox was fitted, operated by a central gear lever; brakes were fully hydraulic and steering of Marles type. As stated earlier, all engine components were of Ford manufacture including the single downdraught carburetter; the engine's 85 bhp produced a top speed of 90 mile/h. Fuel consumption was approximately 18–20 mpg.

1952 Allard 'M2X'

Features: A distinctive and sought-after four-seater car of lively 'two-seater' performance. The Ford V-8 engine advantageous in that spares, reconditioned units etc. are still available (see source below). A sturdy channel and box-section chassis and long-lasting bodywork facilitate renovation. Fully hydraulic brakes fitted. Twin 6v batteries mounted under the front seat, away from vibration. The V-8 engine provides great flexibility in each gear.

Failings: A worn engine will prove very uneconomical (and should be rebuilt.) Ford carburetter spares non-existent now (substitute with large Solex downdraught type or 1948-54 Carter (USA) carburetter.) Twin Ford water-pumps do not give very long service — Kenlowe radiator fan conversion may remedy cooling problems. Bodywork spares only available through breakage.

Allard '21Z Palm Beach'

1952-55. 2¼-litre Sports. 3 seater

The 'Palm Beach 21C' and '21Z' models appeared a year after the introduction of the new Ford 'Consul' and 'Zephyr' saloons in 1951. Outwardly identical in appearance, the more rare '21C' was fitted with a four-cylinder 'Consul' engine, while the '21Z' was powered by a six-cylinder 'Zephyr' unit. The approximate total weight of either model was 1,850 lb., a mere 17 cwt. The '21C' engine, of 1,508cc capacity and 6.8 to 1 compression ratio, developed 47 bhp at 4,400 rev/min. giving a top speed of 80 mile/h, while that of the '21Z' was of 2,267cc capacity and 7 to 1 compression ratio developed 68 bhp at 4,000 rev/min giving a top speed of nearly 100 mile/h. In concept, the 'Palm Beach' two-seater was forward-looking, with neat, economical lines; its design had what was then called 'fully enveloping' alloy bodywork, allied to extreme simplicity and compactness of form. An oval duct with either three horizontal chromed bars or an 'A' motif took the place of a radiator grille, and a full-width frontal aspect blending together the bonnet and front wings, was employed. The headlamps were integral with the front wings, and the small and neat doors, when closed, blended imperceptibly into the overall unified body form. The rear wings, still very open, emerged subtly from a line very close to the rear edges of the doors, this slight accentuation of their form saving the total effect from too much smoothness and monotony of line, and contributing a definitely sporting look. The chassis was of tubular construction. A bench-type seat and central gear lever were provided; all running gear was of Ford manufacture including the three-speed gearbox, hydraulic clutch, prop shaft and rear axle. Fully hydraulic brakes were fitted and the suspension employed coil springs for the divided front axle, with independent coil springs also for the rear. Other Ford manufactured components were the generator, radiator, wheels and steering-wheel. Steering was of Marles pattern. The '21Z' model, with greater flexibility and superior performance was the most impressive; both powerplants were notable in that they were of the 'over square' type, the bore being slightly greater than the stroke. Never a particularly economical engine, the 'Zephyr' unit, providing a mere 23-25 mpg in the Ford 'Zephyr' chassis, gave in contrast 30 mpg in the 'Palm Beach'.

Features: A modern-looking, compact two-seater of high performance and straight-forward design. The use of Ford parts greatly reduces the problem of obtaining spares – Ford 'Zephyr' and 'Consul' models are still far from rare. Either engine may be fitted (fit appropriate prop shaft). Hydraulic clutch progressive for the era. 'Zephyr' engine may be tuned further for higher performance, while kits were originally available to tune the 'Consul' engine into producing 68 bhp at 5,000 rev/min.

Failings: Bodywork spares very hard to trace, perhaps only obtainable through breakage. Ford three-speed column-change gearbox not the ideal design for crisp sports performance, but inadequate. An up-dated 'Pilot' engine would have proved an even more successful power-plant.

Car Club Honorary Secretaries: R.W. May, 8 Paget Close, Horsham, Sussex, RH13 6HD.

Miss P. Hulse, 1 Dalmeny Avenue, Tufnell Park, London, N.7.

SPARES: 1. Many mechanical spares still obtainable through Ford spares stockists.

2. (Ford V-8 'Pilot' reconditioned engines and spares:) M. J. R. Knapman, 46 Morland Road, E. Croydon, Surrey, 01-654 4949.

3. Mechanical spares obtainable through breaking Ford 'Pilots' ('M2X') and 'Zephyrs' ('21Z'.)

4. Through above club.

	Allard 'M2X'	Allard '21 Z, Palm Beach'
Engine (Mechanical)		
No. of cylinders : capacity	V8; 3,622 cc	6; 2,267 cc
Bore and stroke	77·9 x 95·2 mm	79·3 x 76·2 mm
Compression ratio	6·15 : 1	7 : 1
Valve layout	Side	Overhead
Tappet clearances	0.016 in. (cold)	0·014 in. (hot)
Location of valve timing marks	On camshaft wheel	On sprockets
Timing : inlet valve opens	tdc	17° btdc
Piston withdrawal direction	Upwards	Upwards
Engine (Ignition)		
Firing order	1, 5, 4, 8, 6, 3, 7, 2	1, 5, 3, 6, 2, 4
Location of timing marks	None	On crankshaft pulley and front cover
Timing : points open	4° btdc	11° btdc
Original spark plugs	Champion C7	Champion N8B
Plug gap	0.025 in.	0·030–0·034 in.
Original coil	Enfo	Ford
Original distributor	Enfo	Ford
Carburetters		
Original make	Ford	Zenith
Original type	Downdraught	VIG
Choke tube	25 mm	27 mm
Main jet	110	90
Compensating jet	200	100
Slow-running jet	55	55
Pump jet	1-1	70

	Allard 'M2X'	Allard '21Z, Palm Beach'
Electrical Accessories		
Battery	2 x 6v 60 ah	12v 45 ah
Original (Lucas) generator	C45PV/4	Ford 2-brush
Original (Lucas) control box	RB106/1	Ford
Original (Lucas) starter motor	M45G	Ford
Chassis Components and Steering Geometry		
Brakes	Ford-Girling hydraulic	Ford-Girling hydraulic
Rear axle : Type	Spiral bevel	Hypoid bevel
Ratio	3·78 : 1	4·444 : 1
Crown-wheel tooth contact	Adjustable	Adjustable
Front suspension	Coil (divided axle)	Coil (divided axle)
Rear suspension	Transverse leaf	Coils and radius arms
Steering pattern	Marles	Marles
Toe-in	$^3/_{16}$ in.	$^1/_8$ in.
Castor angle	3–4°	3°
Camber angle	2°	2–3°
King-pin inclination	7°	7°
Lubrication		
Engine : Original S.A.E. grade	Summer 30, Winter 20	20
Quantity	8 pt.	6½ pt.
Gearbox : Original S.A.E. grade	90 EP	80 EP
Quantity	2 pt.	2½ pt.
Rear axle : Original S.A.E. grade	90 EP	90 HYP
Quantity	2½ pt.	2½ pt.
Steering box : Original S.A.E. grade	90 EP	80 EP
Tyres		
Size	6·25 x 16	6·40 x 13
Pressures (lb/in²)	F : 24 R : 28	F : 24 R : 24

1953 Allard 'Palm Beach'

Alvis 'TB14'

1950. 2-litre Sports Roadster. 2 seater

1950 Alvis 'TB 14'

The 1937-39 '12/70' chassis served as the basis for the postwar 'TA 14' and 'TB 14' models. The 'TA 14' of 1946 resembled the 'Speed 25' outwardly, the chassis requiring very little modification; components requiring alteration were the exhaust system, leaf-springs, shock-absorbers, rear axle and carburetter, while solid 16in. wheels replaced the 17in. 'knock on' wire wheels of the pre-war '12/70' models. The bore of the cylinders of the prewar engine was increased also, to give a capacity of 1,892cc, the compression ratio being 6.725 to 1; a single SU carburetter was fitted to the 'TA 14' engine. This model had a distinctly '1930s' air (a deliberate continuation of the prewar tradition) and was aimed at the traditionalist British market that existed after the war. Manufactured from 1946-50, fully mechanical brakes were retained at a time when most manufacturers had gone over to at least hydromechanical brake-systems, if not fully hydraulic. In 1950 a small number of 'sports' models appeared, aimed at the export market, and designated 'TB 14'. Also constructed on the '12/70' chassis and using the same engine as the 'TA 14', these 'sports' models broke away completely from the prewar Alvis tradition as regards body styling. Most conspicuous was the large pear-shaped grille which replaced for the first time the radiator shell of all previous models. The completely modern streamlined bodywork, coachbuilt by A. P. Metalcraft, featured headlamps and sidelights integral with the front wings, which were elongated in form and extended to the faces of the rear wings — a contemporary design trend for sports cars. A divided front bumper, solid wheels, heavily chromed adjustable-angle windscreen and large stone-deflectors on the faces of the rear wings were additional features, and the hood could be neatly folded away under a hinged panel behind the seats. The four-cylinder in-line ohv engine, fed by twin SU carburetters, developed 68 bhp at 4,000 rev/min, giving a top speed of 80 mile/h. Fuel consumption was 22-27 mpg. As in the 'TB 14', brakes were fully mechanical and suspension by leaf-springs on all four wheels, but a higher-ratio hypoid rear axle was fitted. An Alvis four-speed '12/70'-type gearbox was installed, operated by a central gear-lever; steering was of Marles pattern.

Features: A distinctive and rather rare car. Alvis engine finely constructed. Lively enough performance coupled with realistic fuel consumption. Orthodox engineering practice throughout, free of snags and eccentricities. Coachbuilt bodywork and interior of finest quality and workmanship. Low compression ratio enables cheaper petrols to be used. Overseas enthusiasts have more likelihood of finding examples of this model in restorable condition.
Failings: Bodywork and chassis demand constant maintenance to ward off corrosion. Body-panel spares virtually non-existent (and this breed of car will not be found in a breaker's yard.) Fully mechanical brakes poor for road conditions in the 1970s. Two carburetters to keep synchronized.

Alvis 'TC 21/100'

1954-55. 3-litre Drophead Coupe. 4 seater

At the March 1950 Geneva Motor Show the 3-litre 'TA 21' appeared as a completely new design. Its sturdy box-section chassis had leaf-spring suspension at the rear, with coil springs for the front wheels, a rubber-mounted anti-roll bar and telescopic shockabsorbers fore and aft. The engine too was a completely new design of six-cylinder in-line ohv pattern, 2,993cc capacity, and of initially 6.9 to 1 compression ratio. The prewar '12/70' gearbox was retained, but brakes were now fully hydraulic. In appearance the 'TA 21' represented a return to a more traditional body design. By 1952 the compression ratio was increased to 7.1 to 1, the original Solex carburetter being replaced first by a single and then twin SUs; also in that year the 'TB 21' appeared, a two-seater similar to the 'TB 14' but incorporating a traditional Alvis radiator shell. In 1953 the 'TC 21' was announced, and at the later 1953 Motor Show the 'TC 21/100' or 'Grey Lady'. This model used the 'TA' gearbox, but a higher ratio hypoid axle and a modified exhaust system, the engine, now of 8 to 1 compression ratio, developing 100 bhp at 4,000 rev/min and giving a top speed of 100 mile/h with 20 mpg. The Mulliner coachbuilt bodywork differed from the 'TC 21' in the inclusion of bonnet scoops and louvres, wire wheels and new window-surrounds; a compromise between traditional angularity and tasteful streamlining, the 'Grey Lady' still remained typically 'Alvis'. Production was cut short in October 1954 when Mulliners were taken over by Standard-Triumph.

Features: Superlative Alvis engineering coupled with Mulliner coachwork. Thoroughly realistic compression ratio for 1970s; fully hydraulic brakes; brisk, silent performance.

Failings: Box-section chassis, though sturdy, must be carefully maintained against corrosion. Body spares very scarce, mechanical spares fairly costly now (for sources, see below.)

Car Club Honorary Secretary: O.N. Trent, 73 Woodmansterne Rd, Coulsdon, Surrey.

SPARES: 1. Red Triangle Autoservices Ltd., Common Lane Trading Estate, Kenilworth, Warwickshire (Kenilworth 57303).
2. 21, Cliffe Lane, Great Harwood, Blackburn, Lancs.
3. (Spares and repairs:) Vintage Racing Cars (Northampton) Ltd.
4. Through above club.

	Alvis 'TB14' Sports	Alvis 'TC 21/100'
Engine (Mechanical)		
No. of cylinders : capacity	4; 1,892 cc	6; 2,993 cc
Bore and stroke	74 x 110 mm	84 x 90 mm
Compression ratio	6·725 : 1	8 : 1
Valve layout	Overhead	Overhead
Tappet clearances	0·009 in. (hot)	0·009 in. (hot)
Location of valve timing marks	On flywheel	On flywheel
Timing : inlet valve opens	15° btdc	20° btdc
Piston withdrawal direction	Downwards	Downwards
Engine (Ignition)		
Firing order	1, 3, 4, 2	1, 5, 3, 6, 2, 4
Location of timing marks	On flywheel	On flywheel
Timing : points open	3–5° btdc	2° btdc
Original spark plugs	Champion L10	Champion L10S
Plug gap	0·022–0·025 in.	0·025 in.
Original (Lucas) coil	B12	B12
Original (Lucas) distributor	DKY4A	DVXH6A
Carburetters		
Original make	2 SU	2 SU
Original type	H4	H4
Choke tube	1½ in.	1½ in.
Metering Needle	DQ	ES
Electrical Accessories		
Battery	12v 63 ah	12v 64 ah
Original (Lucas) generator	C45PV	C45PV
Original (Lucas) control box	RF95/2	RF95/2
Original (Lucas) starter motor	M418G	M45G

1954 Alvis 'TC 21/100'

	Alvis 'TB14' Sports	Alvis 'TC 21/100'
Chassis Components and Steering Geometry		
Brakes	Girling mechanical	Lockheed hydraulic
Rear axle : Type	Hypoid bevel	Hypoid bevel
Ratio	4·3 : 1	3·77 : 1
Crown-wheel tooth contact	Not adjustable	Not adjustable
Front suspension	Semi-elliptic leaf	Independent coil
Rear suspension	Semi-elliptic leaf	Semi-elliptic leaf
Steering pattern	Marles cam and roller	Burman recirculating ball
Toe-in	$1/8$ in.	$1/16$ in. negative
Castor angle	3°	$1\frac{1}{2}$°
Camber angle	$2\frac{1}{2}$°	1°
King-pin inclination	$7\frac{1}{2}$°	9°
Lubrication		
Engine : Original S.A.E. grade	30	20
Quantity	12 pt.	12 pt.
Gearbox : Original S.A.E. grade	30	30
Quantity	3 pt.	3 pt.
Rear axle : Original S.A.E. grade	90HYP	20HYP
Quantity	3 pt.	2 pt.
Steering box : Original S.A.E. grade	90EP	90EP
Tyres		
Size	6·00 x 16	6·00/6·40 x 15
Pressures (lb/in²)	F : 26 R : 26	F : 26 R : 26–30

Armstrong-Siddeley 'Hurricane'

1946-49. 2-litre Sports Roadster. 2-3 seater

1949 Armstrong-Siddeley 'Hurricane'

Designed by Percy Riman, the 'Hurricane' appeared in 1946, being essentially 'prewar' in spirit, with a long bonnet, separate headlamps, open front mudguards and a blunt rear end. The engine, of six-cylinder in-line ohv pattern, 1,991cc capacity and 7 to 1 compression ratio, developed 70 bhp at 4,200 rev/min, giving a top speed in the 80s through a four-speed synchromesh or pre-selector epicyclic gearbox with steering-column lever control. The engine itself was fitted with hydraulic tappets as opposed to the 'solid' type, and a Stromberg downdraught carburetter. A sturdy chassis together with superbly finished bodywork were featured, and the braking system incorporated hydraulic brakes on the front wheels with fully mechanical brakes on the rear (the hydromechanical system.) The preselector gearbox, providing crisp, easy gear changes, was fitted with a centrifugal-type clutch; standard synchromesh gearboxes were fitted with a conventional single-plate clutch, gear selection being by means of a centrally mounted gear lever. Suspension pattern was of independent torsion bars and wishbones for the front wheels, with leaf springs for the rear, the torsion bar suspension on the front wheels adding greatly to the overall smoothness of the ride. Early models employed worm-and-nut steering, later models being equipped with Burman pattern. (By 1949, a new 2.3 litre-engined chassis was offered, forming the basis of both the 'razor edge' Whitley saloon and the new higher-powered 'Hurricane'. The larger engine of this new series was of 2,309cc capacity, developing 75 bhp at 4,200 rev/min. The compression ratio of this unit was lowered to 6.5 to 1; hydraulic tappets were retained.)

Features: A solidly built, 'orthodox British' car of great character. Sturdy chassis, superbly finished bodywork, interior very well appointed. Fairly good fuel consumption (22 mpg) for weight of car.
Failings: Spares difficult. Hydromechanical brakes satisfactory enough, but inferior to fully hydraulic type. Hydraulic tappets less positive than 'solid' tappets (but minimize valve-gear noise.)

Armstrong-Siddeley 'Sapphire 346'

1953-59. 3½-litre Saloon. 4-5 seater

Following on from the 'Eighteens' of 1949-53, the 'Sapphire' was undoubtedly intended as a prestige car; by 1956 it cost £1,928. It could be purchased with a Wilson pre-selector gearbox, if preferred. As in so many of these postwar models, traditional angularity was combined with a moderate amount of streamlining; the straightness of the radiator grille was now subtly curved — and this tendency was gracefully echoed throughout in a very tasteful way. Headlamps, no longer separate, were fully blended into the wings. The general lines of the body were crisper towards the window and roof area, while more flowing over the wings and boot. The 1953 model had a six-cylinder in-line engine of 3,435 cc, giving 120 bhp at 4,200 rev/min. By 1956 the engine was producing 125 bhp at 4,700 rev/min. Maximum speed in the highest of the four gears was just over 90 mile/h. At the cruising speed of 70 mile/h fuel consumption was 20 mpg. Steering was of Burman recirculating ball pattern and was low-geared and heavy. Brakes, however, were of servo-assisted hydraulic type and very efficient. The suspension pattern consisted of independent coil for the front wheels and leaf-springs for the rear. The gear-lever was mounted on the steering column. The cheapest version had a single Stromberg carburetter and manual gearbox; more costly versions offered twin carburetters and bucket-type front seats. The degree of finish was excellent throughout.

Features: A luxury car of very high quality. Smooth, effortless motoring. The engine will give long service.

Failings: Prone to rusting in lower bodywork and box-sections. High fuel consumption. Heavy clutch. Wide turning-circle and heavy steering. Indecisive gearchange. All spares very expensive.

Car Club Honorary Secretary: J.D. Hubbuck, 90 Alumnhurst Road, Bournemouth, Hants.

SPARES: (1) Motolympia, Welshpool, Montgomeryshire (Welshpool 2327).
             (2) Through above club.

1953 Armstrong-Siddeley 'Sapphire 346'

	Armstrong-Siddeley 'Hurricane'	Armstrong-Siddeley 'Sapphire 346'
Engine (Mechanical)		
No. of cylinders : capacity	6; 1,991 cc	6; 3435 cc
Bore and stroke	65 x 100 mm	90 x 90 mm
Compression ratio	7 : 1	7 : 1
Valve layout	Overhead	Overhead
Tappet clearances	0.075 in. withhydraulic tappets dry (hot)	0.006 in. (hot)
Location of valve timing marks	On camshaft and crankshaft sprocket boss	On camshaft and crankshaft sprocket boss
Timing : inlet valve opens	10° btdc	8° btdc
Piston withdrawal direction	Downwards	Upwards

	Armstrong-Siddeley 'Hurricane'	Armstrong-Siddeley 'Sapphire 346'
Engine (Ignition)		
Firing order	1, 5, 3, 6, 2, 4	1, 5, 3, 6, 2, 4
Location of timing marks	On flywheel ring and housing	Crankshaft pulley and timing cover
Timing : points open	$10^°$ btdc	$5^°$ btdc
Original spark plugs	Champion L10	Lodge CLN H
Plug gap	0·018 in.	0·028—0·033 in.
Original (Lucas) coil	Q12	B12
Original (Lucas) distributor	DX6A (C43)	DM6
Carburetters		
Original make	Stromberg downdraught	Stromberg downdraught
Original type	Preselector — DAV-36	DAA-36
	Synchromesh — DBVA-36	
Choke tube	$1^1/_{32}$ in.	$1^3/_{16}$ in.
Main jet	0·049 in.	0·058 in.
Electrical Accessories		
Battery	12v 51 ah	12v 64 ah
Original (Lucas) generator	C45PV/3	C45PV/5
Original (Lucas) control box	RF91	RB106/1
Original (Lucas) starter motor	M418G	M45G
Chassis Components and Steering Geometry		
Brakes	Girling hydromechanical	Girling hydraulic with Vac-Hydro servo
Rear axle : Type	Hypoid bevel	Hypoid bevel
Ratio	5·1 : 1	4·09 : 1
Crown-wheel tooth contact	Adjustable by shims	Adjustable by shims
Front suspension	Torsion bars	Independent coil
Rear suspension	Semi-elliptic leaf	Semi-elliptic leaf
Steering pattern	1945-47 Worm and nut	Burman recirculating ball
	1948-49 Burman	
Toe-in	$^3/_{16}$ in.	$^3/_{16}$ in.
Castor angle	$1^°$	$1^°$ (laden)
Camber angle	$2\frac{1}{2}^°$	$2^°$
King-pin inclination	$7\frac{1}{2}^°$	$5\frac{1}{2}^°$
Lubrication		
Engine : Original S.A.E. grade	Summer 40, Winter 30	Summer 30, Winter 20
Quantity	11 pt. + 2 pt. filter	11 pt. + 1 pt. filter
Gearbox : Original S.A.E. grade	Preselector — 30, Synchromesh — 40	Preselector — 30, Synchromesh —40
Quantity	Preselector — 4pt. Synchromesh — 3½ pt.	Preselector — 6pt. Synchromesh — 5 pt.
Rear axle : Original S.A.E. grade	90 HYP	90 HYP
Quantity	2½ pt.	2½ pt.
Steering box : Original S.A.E. grade	140EP	90HYP
Tyres		
Size	5·50 x 17	6·70 x 16
Pressures (lb/in^2)	F : 26 R : 26	F : 24 R : 24

1950 Aston Martin '2-Litre' or 'DB 1'

Aston Martin '2-Litre'

1948-50. 2-litre Sports. 2 seater

Just before the war, Aston Martin decided they should develop a new power unit; the prewar engines had remained practically the same over a long period *i.e.* of four-cylinder ohc pattern and 1½-litre, later enlarged to 2-litre, capacity. Hence during the war years there emerged a new design, this time a pushrod overhead-valve engine; at the same time, a new chassis was evolved in a 'one-off' experimental car named the 'Atom', which was run from 1940 onwards. The chassis used in this car was a completely new concept, employing independent coil front suspension and a saloon body-frame welded up from small box-section tubes. As fate would have it, 1947 saw a take-over by the David Brown group, which also merged Aston Martin with Lagonda Cars Ltd., Tickfords being absorbed a while later. Hence under the David Brown aegis was combined the potential of three very remarkable companies. Nevertheless, for the time being, work continued on the postwar prototype utilizing the new two-litre engine and chassis, and in 1948 the new '2-Litre' model appeared, to be known later as the 'DB 1'. The engine, of 1,970cc capacity and 7.25 to 1 compression ratio, developed 90 bhp at 4,750 rev/min, giving a top speed in the region of 90-100 mile/h. Features of the engine were the redesigned combustion-spaces in the cylinder head and vertical inlet with inclined exhaust valves, giving unhindered flow of the exhaust gases. The exhaust valve seats were also directly water-cooled. Carburation was by twin SUs; the crankshaft was massive and had five bearings; there was a finned sump, cast in alloy. In external appearance the 'DB 1' was

90

very modern for the time: the streamlined, enveloping bodywork was made up from aluminium panels, the aerodynamic curves of the bonnet and front wings sweeping back from a bolder yet basically traditional radiator grille, continuing at the rear in gracefully faired-in rear wings. The spare wire wheel was housed inside one of the front wings, the entire front section forward of the scuttle hinging upwards to reveal the engine and front chassis. A four-speed gearbox and fully hydraulic brakes were fitted. A total of only 15 'DB 1's were built.

Features: A very rare, high performance car. Alloy bodywork and 'tubular-type' chassis, if maintained, could give indefinitely long service.
Failings: Engine spares difficult to obtain, bodywork spares unobtainable. Performance definitely inferior to the 'DB 2'; nonetheless, a very distinctive and sought-after car.

Aston Martin 'DB2'

1950-54. 2½-litre Sports Saloon. 2-3 seater

The short-lived 'DB 1' was soon to give way to a new and more powerful model, the prototype for which ran in the Le Mans of 1949. To be called the 'DB 2', it consisted basically of the 'DB 1' chassis powered by a 2½-litre Lagonda engine, the body being a new 2-door saloon developed from the aerodynamic form of the 'DB 1'. The six-cylinder engine (for more details, see the Lagonda section) came in two forms: (1) the 'Standard' type of 6.5 to 1 compression ratio, or (2) the 'Vantage', a modified version with high-compression pistons giving a compression ratio of 8.2 to 1. Both being of 2,580cc capacity, the 'Standard' engine developed 105 bhp at 5,000 rev/min, while the 'Vantage' produced 125 bhp at 5,000 rev/min, giving a top speed of 115-120 mile/h. As to the body styling, there were departures from that of the 'DB 1': a single integral form now embraced both the front and rear wings on either side, the door panels being cut out of this unified shape. The headlamps and sidelights were integral also with the faces of the front wings, the curving bonnet sloping back from a radiator grille which at first was identical to that of the 'DB 1', but which was soon replaced by an aluminium one-piece grille in the shape of an inverted T. The flowing lines of the front section were continued at the rear in a 'fast' back; wire wheels were fitted. Excellent engine accessibility was once more afforded in the same way as in the '2-litre'. Bodywork was in aluminium, a central steel panel being laminated with a layer of fibreglass wool between the steel and the alloy, acting as a heat- and sound-proof insulator in the area of the firewall. Suspension was by coil springs on all four wheels, and there was a choice of column- or floor-change gear levers for the four-speed David Brown gearbox. Brakes were fully hydraulic. The interior was also beautifully finished.

Features: As for 'DB 1'; Lagonda engine far more easy to service or rebuild, spares for this being more readily available. This model plus 'Vantage' engine affords breathtaking performance.

1951 Aston Martin 'DB 2'

Failings: Very few, although certain mechanical spares are now becoming difficult to trace. Bodywork spares only obtainable through breakage.

Car Club Honorary Secretary: K.L. Fuller, 'Conifers', The Way, Reigate, Surrey, RH2 0LB.

SPARES: Through Aston Martin Club, or Lagonda Club (for engine spares,) — Aston Martin Lagonda Ltd no longer able to assist.

	Aston Martin '2-Litre' ('DB 1')	Aston Martin 'DB 2'
Engine (Mechanical)		
No. of cylinders : capacity	4; 1,970 cc	6; 2,580 cc
Bore and stroke	82·5 x 92 mm	78 x 90 mm
Compression ratio	7·25 : 1	'Standard' engine 6·5 : 1 'Vantage' engine 8·2 : 1
Valve layout	Overhead	Overhead (dohc)
Tappet clearances	0·010 in. (cold)	Inlet 0·011–0·013 in. Exhaust 0.013–0.014 in. (cold)
Location of valve timing marks	—	Camshaft sprocket marks adjacent and in line
Timing : inlet valve opens	10° btdc	10° btdc
Piston withdrawal direction	Upwards	Upwards
Engine (Ignition)		
Firing order	1, 3, 4, 2	1, 5, 3, 6, 2, 4
Location of timing marks	—	On flywheel
Timing : points open	—	10° btdc, retarded
Original spark plugs	Lodge HNP	K.L.G. P10 L.30 or P10 L.70
Plug gap	0·020 in.	0·022 in.
Original (Lucas) coil	B12	B12-1
Original (Lucas) distributor	DVX4A	DVXH6A

	Aston Martin '2-Litre' ('DB 1')	Aston Martin 'DB 2'
Carburetters		
Original make	2 SU	2 SU
Original type	H4T	H4T or H6
Choke tube	1½ in.	1½ in. (H4T) or 1¾ in. (H6)
Metering needle	ER	GB (H4T) or RJ (H6)
Electrical Accessories		
Battery	12v 64 ah	12v 64 ah
Original (Lucas) generator	RA5	C45PV/S-5
Original (Lucas) control box	RF95/2	RF95 (later RB 106/1)
Original (Lucas) starter motor	M45G	M45G.L7
Chassis Components and Steering Geometry		
Brakes	Girling hydraulic	Girling hydraulic (2 LS)
Rear axle : Type	Hypoid bevel	Hypoid bevel
Ratio	4·1 : 1	3·77 : 1
Crown-wheel tooth contact	Adjustable by shims	Adjustable by shims
Front suspension	Coil springs and trailing links	Coil springs and trailing links
Rear suspension	Coil springs and parallel radius arms	Coil springs and parallel radius arms
Steering pattern	Worm and double roller	Worm and double roller
Toe-in	⅛ in.	⅛ in.
Castor angle	2¼°	2¼°
Camber angle	2¾°	2¾°
King-pin inclination	Nil	Nil
Lubrication		
Engine : Original S.A.E. grade	40	Summer 40, Winter 30
Quantity	12 pt.	15 pt.
Gearbox : Original S.A.E. grade	90	30
Quantity	2¼ pt.	2¼ pt.
Rear axle : Original S.A.E. grade	90HYP	90HYP
Quantity	2 pt.	2 pt.
Steering box : Original S.A.E. grade	90EP	90EP
Tyres		
Size	5·75 x 16	5·75 x 16 or 6·00 x 16
Pressures (lb/in^2)	F : 27 R : 27	F : 26 R : 27

Aston Martin 'DB 2' chassis

Austin A90 'Atlantic'

1948-52. 2½-litre Sports Saloon. 4 seater

1951 Austin A.90 'Atlantic'

As its name implies, the A.90 'Atlantic' was designed primarily to attract the North American export market. Compared to its Austin contemporaries (the A.40 'Dorset' and 'Devon', and the A.70 'Hampshire' and 'Hereford') its body styling was certainly revolutionary and very eye-catching. The side aspect of the front wings and lower rear was virtually an aerofoil section; the rounded bulbous front wings blended into the bonnet and grille, their lines producing a streamlined flow over the scuttle, that continued to a tapered point over the rear wheels. The front wheels were exposed openly in the front wings, whereas the rear wings, as such, were non-existent and blended fully into the lower rear section. Under the flowing lines of the bonnet was a four-cylinder ohv engine of 2,660cc fitted with twin SU carburetters, delivering 88 bhp at 4,000 rev/min and giving a crisp performance throughout the four gears, with a top speed in the 90s. The gear-change was column-mounted. Steering was of Burman Douglas cam-and-lever type (general Austin practice.) Suspension on the front wheels was independent coil, with leaf-springs on the rear. Leather upholstery was standard. A true chassis was incorporated of welded box-section, with central cross bracing. Brakes were hydromechanical. This same engine was used in the Austin-Healey '100' and '100M' (modified).

Features: An outstandingly 'different' design as regards body shape. Powerful, sprightly, yet orthodox engine. Spares through British Leyland, to some degree.
Failings: Fuel consumption rather high. Brake design barely adequate for 1970s. Body will tend to corrode; chassis needs maintenance.

Car Club Honorary Secretary: A.D. Easen, Valetta, Bighton Lane,
Bishops Sutton, Alresford, Hants.

SPARES: 1. Through British Leyland.
2. (Engine:) F. Depper, 19, Whitmore Rd., Whitnash, Leamington Spa, Warwicks (Austin-Healey '100' specialist).
3. Motolympia, Welshpool, Montgomeryshire (Welshpool 2327).
4. Through above club.

Austin A.90 'Atlantic'

Engine (Mechanical)	
No. of cylinders : capacity	4; 2,660 cc
Bore and stroke	87·3 x 111·1 mm
Compression ratio	7·5 : 1
Valve layout	Overhead
Tappet clearances	0.015 in. (later 0.012 in.) (hot or cold)
Location of valve timing marks	Spot-marked gears
Timing : inlet valve opens	5° btdc
Piston withdrawal direction	Upwards

Engine (Ignition)	
Firing order	1, 3, 4, 2
Location of timing marks	On flywheel
Timing : points open	6° btdc
Original spark plugs	Champion NA8
Plug gap	0.022
Original (Lucas) coil	B12
Original (Lucas) distributor	DM2

Carburetters	
Original make	2 SU
Original type	Front H4T, Rear H4

Electrical Accessories	
Battery	12v 64 ah
Original (Lucas) generator	C45PV/5
Original (Lucas) control box	RF95/2
Original (Lucas) starter motor	M418G

Chassis Components and Steering Geometry		Lubrication	
Brakes	Girling hydromechanical	Engine : Original S.A.E. grade	30
		Quantity	12 pt.
Rear axle : Type	Spiral bevel	Gearbox : Original S.A.E. grade	40
Ratio	3·667 : 1	Quantity	3 pt.
Crown-wheel tooth contact	Adjustable by shims	Rear axle : Original S.A.E. grade	140 EP
Front suspension	Independent coil	Quantity	2¾ pt.
Rear suspension	Semi-elliptic leaf	Steering box : Original S.A.E. grade	140 EP
Steering pattern	Cam and lever		
Toe-in	$^1/_{16}$ — $^1/_8$ in.	Tyres	
Castor angle	1¼°	Size	5·50 x 16
Camber angle	1°	Pressures (lb/in^2)	F : 25-26
King-pin inclination	6½°		R : 25-29

Austin-Healey '100'

1953-55; 2½-litre Sports Roadster. 2 seater

The Donald Healey Motor Company amalgamated with the Austin Motor Company in 1952, and this was announced at the Earls Court Motor Show of that year. Hence the prototype Healey '100' was re-named the Austin-Healey '100' overnight. The design team, led by Donald Healey and including his son Geoffrey, had, a year before, discarded the original chassis design used since 1946 and formulated a completely new type. This new chassis had box-section side members braced by parallel and cruciform cross-members also of box-section; other features made the chassis a compromise between separate-chassis and unit construction. The suspension employed coil-and-wishbone for the front wheels, with leaf-springs for

1953 Austin-Healey '100'. The designer is sitting in the (r.h.) passenger seat

the rear. As for the power unit, this was basically an Austin A.90 'Atlantic' engine of four-cylinder-in-line ohv pattern and 2,660cc capacity, and so the amalgamation with Austins was opportune. This engine developed 90 bhp at 4,000 rev/min, top speed of the '100' being 111 mile/h. But without doubt it was the body shape which was so sensational — a classic design which came into its own once the hood was folded away; the smooth graceful lines from radiator grille to boot produced an efficient, aerodynamic and aesthetically beautiful effect. The wings remained open to expose both front and rear wire wheels; the radiator grille, an inverted triangle, was situated below the level of the front wings; the tiny windscreen could be raked back at a steep angle. A three-speed gearbox with overdrive, and fully hydraulic brakes were fitted. Bodywork was of pressed steel, and the model was designated the code BN1, distinguishing it from the four-speed gearbox and hypoid axle of the BN2 of 1955.

Features: Excellent performance, timeless body design. Spares still obtainable through specialists (see below). Fanatically keen car clubs.
Failings: Well-used examples offered for sale may have been 'thrashed'. Steel bodywork, particularly that adjacent to box-section chassis, demands constant preservation against corrosion.

Austin-Healey '100S'

1955. 2½-litre Sports Racer. 2 seater

The '100' model, although very successful from the outset, proved to be slightly inadequate in competition events. Hence an improved design, the '100 S', went into production for a few months during 1955, featuring alloy bodywork, a smaller and now oval radiator grille, a louvred bonnet top, a one-piece perspex windscreen, and several weight-saving omissions to give an overall reduction of 220 lb. But it was the engine modifications which were the most significant feature, and a kit was offered to '100' owners to enable them to convert their engine into the '100 S' type. The modifications consisted of fitting an entirely new alloy cylinder-head, twin 1¾ in. SU carburetters, a high-lift camshaft, 8.3 to 1 compression ratio pistons, and a twin exhaust system. The modified engine produced 132 bhp at 4,700 rev/min, and top speed of the '100 S' was 125 mile/h. A four speed gearbox without overdrive was fitted, and the standard hypoid rear axle ratio was 2.92 to 1. The suspension was of the BN2 type (independent coil front, leaf-springs rear) but with the BN2's longer coil springs complemented by stiffer spring settings and double-acting shock-absorbers. Dunlop disc brakes were fitted on all four wheels. (In 1955 the '100 M' model became available also, being virtually a '100' BN2 fitted with a '100 S' engine, i.e. with steel bodywork, not alloy. Top speed here was 115 mile/hr.)

Features: Superlative performance, beautiful design throughout; alloy bodywork can last indefinitely. Engine spares still obtainable through specialist (see below).

Failings: Only fifty '100S' models built, so availability of surplus body spares will be nil by now. Also most models were exported. (Perhaps USA enthusiasts will find the task of restoration easier.) '100 M' restoration-conversion might prove a satisfactory compromise.

Car Club Honorary Secretary: I. Picton-Robinson, 12 Boxnott Close, Webheath, Redditch, Worcs.

'100-4' Register: R. Francis, 117 Rowton Drive, Streetly, Sutton Coldfield, Warwicks.

SPARES: F. Depper, 19 Whitmore Rd, Whitnash, Leamington Spa, Warwicks.
('100' fibreglass wings, boot lids, sills:) P.M.A. Accessories Ltd., 30-31, Tudor Chambers, Station Rd, Wood Green, London N.22.

	Austin-Healey '100'	Austin-Healey '100 S'
Engine (Mechanical)		
No. of cylinders : capacity	4; 2,660 cc	4; 2,660 cc
Bore and stroke	87·3 x 111 mm	87·3 x 111 mm
Compression ratio	7·5 : 1	8·3 : 1
Valve layout	Overhead	Overhead
Tappet clearances	0·012 in.	0·015 in.
Location of valve timing marks	Spots on gears	Spots on gears
Timing : inlet valve opens	5° btdc	10° btdc
Piston withdrawal direction	Upwards	Upwards
Engine (Ignition)		
Firing order	1, 3, 4, 2	1, 3, 4, 2
Location of timing marks	None	None
Timing : points open	6° btdc	–
Original spark plugs	Champion NA8	Champion NA10
Plug gap	0·025 in.	0.025 in.
Original (Lucas) coil	B12	–
Original (Lucas) distributor	DM2P4	–
Carburetters		
Original make	2 SU	2 SU
Original type	H4	H6
Choke tube	–	1¾ in.
Jet size	0·090	0·100
Metering needle	QW, or QA (rich)	KW1 or KW (rich)
Electrical Accessories		
Battery	2 x 6v 50 ah	2 x 6v 38 ah
Original (Lucas) generator	C45PV/5	–
Original (Lucas) control box	RB106	–
Original (Lucas) starter motor	M418G	–
Chassis Components and Steering Geometry		
Brakes	Girling hydraulic	Dunlop disc
Rear axle : Type	Spiral bevel	Hypoid bevel
Ratio	4·125 : 1	2·92 : 1
Crown-wheel tooth contact	(No adjustment details)	
Front suspension	Independent coil	Independent coil
Rear suspension	Semi-elliptic leaf	Semi-elliptic leaf
Steering Pattern	Cam and peg	Cam and peg
Toe-in	1/16 – 1/8 in.	1/8 in.
Castor angle	1¾°	–
Camber angle	1°	–
King-pin inclination	6½°	–

1955 Austin-Healey '100 S'

	Austin-Healey '100'		Austin-Healey '100 S'	
Lubrication				
Engine : Original S.A.E. grade	Summer 30, Winter 20		Racing grade	
Quantity	11¾ pt.		11¾ pt.	
Gearbox : Original S.A.E. grade	30		—	
Quantity	5½ pt. inc. overdrive		3 pt.	
Rear axle : Original S.A.E. grade	140EP		90HYP	
Quantity	2¼ pt.		2½ pt.	
Steering box : Original S.A.E. grade	140 EP		140 EP	
Tyres				
Size	5·90 x 15		5·50 x 15	
Pressures (lb/in^2)	F : 20	R : 23	F : 23	R : 26

Bristol '400', '401', '402'

1947-53. 2-litre Sports Saloon. 4-5 seater

Manufactured by the Car Division of the Bristol Aircraft Company, postwar Bristol '400's may be said to be virtually carbon-copies of the prewar German BMW '327' Sports Cabriolet of 1939 as regards body design, and the BMW '328' two-seater Sports of 1937 as regards the engine. The original Bristol engine, designated the code '85', and later units prefixed '85A', '85B' and '85C' were all of six-cylinder ohv pattern and 1,971cc capacity, of 7.5 to 1 compression ratio and of identical bore, stroke and capacity to the '328' engine. As a comparison, the engine of the 1949 Bristol '400' developed 85 bhp at 4,500 rev/min giving a top speed of 95 mile/h, whereas the 1939 BMW '327', with a similar overall dry weight and engine very similar to the '328' developing 80 bhp at 4,500 rev/min, had a top speed of 93 mile/h. (The 1937 '328', because of its much reduced total weight, could top 100 mile/h). Three SU carburetters were fitted to the earlier Bristol engines, with a change to three 'Solex' carburetters on '85C' types. In body design Bristols clung very closely to BMW prewar trends, (albeit forward-

1951 Bristol '401'

looking), where streamlining of the bonnet, wings and other bodywork engendered curved flowing lines, in contrast to the more angular styles still prevalent. The bodywork was of aluminium and the chassis a tubular steel structure. Fully hydraulic brakes were fitted, together with rack-and-pinion steering; suspension was by transverse leaf-spring and wishbone for the front wheels and by torsion bars for the rear. The '401' model had a very different body design from the '400', the front wings being flatter, the 'fastback' more pronounced and the whole appearance smoother and less influenced by prewar BMW practice. This trend continued in the '402', (a convertible version, of which only six were made). Constructed on the superleggra principle, the alloy bodywork of the '401' was attached over a framework of fine steel tubes.

Features: The whole car superbly built throughout. Alloy body panels. Engine built to very fine tolerances. Three carburetters an added refinement regarding tuning and performance.

Failings: Engine spares costly. Very few real failings, except that three carburetters need to be kept synchronized, and if worn will prove costly to replace. Box section chassis demands regular maintenance.

	Bristol '400', '401', '402'	Bristol '403', '404', '405'
Engine (Mechanical)		
No. of cylinders : capacity	6; 1,971 cc	6; 1,971 cc
Bore and stroke	66 x 96 mm	66 x 96 mm
Compression ratio	7·5 : 1	8·5 : 1
Valve layout	Overhead inclined	Overhead inclined
Tappet clearances	0.010 in. (cold)	0.012 in. (cold)
Location of valve timing marks	On flywheel	On flywheel
Timing : inlet valve opens	10° btdc	15° btdc
Piston withdrawal direction	Piston upwards, rod downwards	Piston upwards, rod downwards
Engine (Ignition)		
Firing order	1, 5, 3, 6, 2, 4	1, 5, 3, 6, 2, 4
Location of timing marks	On flywheel	On flywheel
Timing : points open	tdc	tdc
Original spark plugs	K.L.G. PT. L70	K.L.G. PT. L80
Plug gap	0·018 in.	0·018 in.
Original (Lucas) coil	B 12	B 12
Original (Lucas) distributor	DX6A	—
Carburettors	85 engine — 3 Solex	
Original make	85A & 85B — 3 SU	85 C engine — 3 Solex
Original type	Solex : 30AAPI, SU : D2	32 B1
Choke tube	Solex : 22, SU : —	24
Main jet	Solex : 110, SU : 85A — Needle FH 85B — Needle FK	110
Correction jet	Solex : 270, SU : —	230
Pilot jet	Solex : 55-GA5, SU : —	50-GA2
Electrical Accessories		
Battery	12v 51 ah	12v 51 ah
Original (Lucas) generator	C45PV	C45PV
Original (Lucas) control box	RF95/2	RF95/2
Original (Lucas) starter motor	M35G/1	M35G/1

	Bristol '400', '401', '402'	Bristol '403', '404', '405'
Chassis Components and Steering Geometry		
Brakes	Lockheed hydraulic	Lockheed hydraulic
Rear axle : Type	Spiral bevel	Spiral bevel
Ratio	3·9 : 1	4·22 : 1
Crown-wheel tooth contact	Adjustable screwed sleeves or shims	Adjustable screwed sleeves or shims
Front suspension	Transverse leaf spring & wishbone	Transverse leaf spring & wishbone
Rear suspension	Torsion bars	Torsion bars
Steering Pattern	Rack and pinion	Rack and pinion
Toe-in	0–⅛ in.	0–⅛ in.
Castor angle	2–2¾°	2–2¾°
Camber angle	0–1°	0–1°
King-pin inclination	5° 18′	5° 18′
Lubrication		
Engine : Original S.A.E. grade	Summer 50, Winter 30	Summer 30, Winter 20
Quantity	10 pt.	12 pt.
Gearbox : Original S.A.E. grade	50	50 ('405' : 30)
Quantity	3 pt.	3 pt. ('405' 3½ pt. with overdrive)
Rear axle : Original S.A.E. grade	140 EP	140 EP
Quantity	4 pt.	3 pt.
Steering box : Original S.A.E. grade	Central (one-shot) lubricator	Central (one-shot) lubricator
Tyres		403 : 5·75 x 16
Size	5.75 x 16	404 : 5.50 x 16
		405 : 5·75 x 16
Pressures (lb/in²)	F : '400' : 26, '401' : 22, '402' : 22	F : '403' : 22, '404' : 24, '405' : 27
	R : '400' : 26, '401' : 26, '402' : 26	R : '403' : 26, '404' : 27, '405' : 30

Bristol '403', '404', '405'

1953-58. 2-litre Sports Saloon/Coupé. 2 or 4 seater

The '403' had a higher-powered engine than the '402', together with a remote-controlled central gear lever. In September 1953 the '404' Coupé appeared, the body shape having changed radically to fit in more with the trends of the times: (integral form of front and rear wings, recessed grille with the bonnet blending into the overall frontal section, one-piece windscreen, rejection of the idea of an 'open' car, 'fast' back.) The '403' engine remained basically the same as that fitted in the '400', '401' and '402'. Subtle modifications raised the power until by 1954 this same powerplant was developing 125 bhp at 5,500 rev/min, top speed then being 118 mile/h. Bristols did not succumb to the fashion for wire wheels, but retained the solid type of wheel perforated by brake-cooling holes. The overall finish of all the models was excellent throughout. These later models employed a lower rear axle ratio, this latter being still of the obsolescent spiral bevel type. Three carburetters were retained, as in the earlier models, but

1954 Bristol '404'

Solex were substituted for the SUs. Fully hydraulic brakes were fitted, suspension being identical to that of the '400', '401' and '402'; steering was of rack-and-pinion design. The '405', the only four-door Bristol manufactured, used the '403's chassis and mechanics, its less streamlined bodywork being constructed on an ash frame.

Features: As for '400', '401', '402'.
Failings: As for '400', '401', '402'; '405's wooden body-frame can decay.
Car Club Honorary Secretary: F. J. T. Hewitt, 5 St. Leonard's Court, East Sheen, London, S.W.14.
SPARES: (1) Bristol Cars Ltd, (low on '400' spares) Filton, Bristol. (0272 693831)
   (2) Anthony Crook Motors Ltd, Chiswick Flyover, Gt West Road, London W.4. (01 994 3417)
   (3) R.F. Fuggle Ltd, 125 High Road, Bushey, Herts. (01 950 1685)
   (4) Through above club.

1952 Daimler '3-Litre Coupé'

Daimler '3-litre Coupé'

1952-53. Convertible Coupé. 4-5 seater

Introduced in 1952, and rather short-lived, the 3-litre 'Coupé' was intended specifically for long-distance high-speed travel and was fitted with a 'Regency' engine modified with a higher 7.5 to 1 compression ratio aluminium cylinder-head. This unit, of 2,952cc capacity, produced 100 bhp at 4,200 rev/min, giving a top speed of over 90 mile/h. The body design was a beautiful compromise between the Daimler tradition and the onset of tasteful streamlining. The upright Daimler radiator of prewar days had become subtly curved; from the high, straight lines of the bonnet top, the rest of the design flowed gracefully into smoothly-cowled bulbous wings and a classic body form. Most noticeable was the way the elongated line of the front wings was taken up again as the origin of the rear wings, which incorporated wheel spats of a uniquely 'correct', tasteful, yet inspired shape. The headlamps and sidelights were fully blended into the front wings, and a curving one-piece windscreen was used. Twin 8-gallon fuel tanks were fitted, one in each rear wing. The hood and windows were power-operated, as was the lid of the large-capacity boot. A fluid flywheel and four-speed pre-selector gearbox was fitted, operated by a column-mounted gear lever. A very rugged chassis was employed, together with steel bodywork, the general standard of exterior and interior finish being superlative. The choice of a two-tone colour scheme also complemented very successfully the superb overall effect.

1952 Daimler '3-Litre Coupé'

Features: Beautiful engineering and craftsmanship throughout. Smooth, silent power-transfer; high cruising speed may be maintained for long periods, in complete comfort.

Failings: Both chassis and bodywork demand regular maintenance to ward off corrosion. Rather high fuel consumption. All spares now very scarce and costly, if not unobtainable.

Daimler 'Straight Eight'

1946-53. 5½-litre Limousine. 6 seater

Daimlers used an eight-cylinder in-line pushrod overhead-valve engine of 5,460cc and 6.5 to 1 compression ratio to power this prestige limousine. This unit developed 150 bhp at 3,600 rev/min, giving a very comfortable top speed of 95 mile/h. General interior and exterior finish was, of course, excellent; the bodywork was by Hooper. Brakes were Daimler-Girling hydromechanical (hydraulic front, mechanical rear) and suspension pattern independent coil for the front wheels, with leaf-springs for the rear. A four-speed pre-selector gearbox with column-mounted gear lever and fluid flywheel was fitted, as generally favoured by Daimlers. Seating accommodation was very spacious indeed. The total price of the 'Straight Eight' was in fact slightly higher than its contemporary, the Rolls-Royce 'Silver Dawn' Sports Saloon.

Features: If still in reasonable condition, the massive slow-revving engine could give many years of further service. All bodywork was of supreme quality — corrosion should be minimal on well-maintained examples. A very sturdy chassis fitted.

Failings: High fuel consumption (10-12 mpg). Engine spares non-existent, and engine rebuild would be very costly indeed. Two massive 6v 110ah batteries to replace, if deteriorated. Starter motor small for a 5½-litre engine (in winter conditions).

Car Club Honorary Secretary: H.D. Saunders, Eastgate House, Top Street, Appleby Magna, nr. Burton-on-Trent, Staffs.

SPARES: 1. Through above club.
2. Motolympia, Welshpool, Montgomeryshire (Welshpool 2327).

1951 Daimler 'Straight Eight' Limousine

	Daimler '3-Litre Coupe'	Daimler 'Straight Eight'
Engine (Mechanical)		
No. of cylinders : capacity	6; 2,952 cc	8; 5,460 cc
Bore and stroke	76·2 x 108 mm	85·1 x 120 mm
Compression ratio	7·5 : 1	6·3 : 1
Valve layout	Overhead	Overhead
Tappet clearances	0.013 in. (hot)	0.015 in. (hot)
Location of valve timing marks	Hole in timing wheel	On chainwheel and flywheel
Timing : inlet valve opens	13° btdc	22° btdc
Piston withdrawal direction	Upwards	Piston upwards, rod downwards
Engine (Ignition)		
Firing order	1, 5, 3, 6, 2, 4	1, 6, 2, 5, 8, 3, 7, 4
Location of timing marks	On flywheel	On flywheel ring
Timing : points open	7° btdc	5° btdc
Original spark plugs	Lodge CB14	Lodge CB14
Plug gap	0·020 in.	0·030 in.
Original (Lucas) coil	B12	B12
Original (Lucas) distributor	DVX6A	—
Carburetters		
Original make	2 SU	2 SU
Original type	H4	—
Choke tube	—	1½ in.
Metering needle	No. 5	FB
Electrical Accessories		
Battery	12v 64 ah	2 x 6v 110 ah
Original (Lucas) generator	C45PV/5	C45PV/3
Original (Lucas) control box	RB106	RJF91
Original (Lucas) starter motor	M418G	M418G
Chassis Components and Steering Geometry		
Brakes	Daimler-Girling hydromechanical	Daimler-Girling hydromechanical
Rear axle : Type	Hypoid bevel	Hypoid bevel
Ratio	3·46 : 1	4·1 : 1
Crown-wheel tooth contact	Adjustable by shims and screw	Adjustable by screw and washers
Front suspension	Independent coil	Independent coil and wishbone
Rear suspension	Semi-elliptic leaf	Semi-elliptic leaf
Steering pattern	Worm and double roller	Worm and double roller
Toe-in	$1/8 - 3/16$ in.	$1/8 - 3/16$ in.
Castor angle	1½°	3/8 in. trail
Camber angle	1½°	1½°
King-pin inclination	7½°	6°
Lubrication		
Engine : Original S.A.E. grade	30	30
Quantity	12½ pt.	26 pt.
Gearbox : Original S.A.E. grade	30 (Flywheel : 30)	30 (Flywheel 30)
Quantity	4pt. (Flywheel : 9¾ pt.)	8 pt. (Flywheel 9¾ pt.)
Rear axle : Original S.A.E. grade	90 HYP	90 HYP
Quantity	3 pt.	8 pt.
Steering box : Original S.A.E. grade	140 EP	140 EP
Tyres		
Size	6·50 x 16	8·00 x 17
Pressures (lb/in²)	F : 28 R : 30	F : 34 R : 36

Ford V-8 'Pilot'

1947-51. 3½-litre Saloon. 5 seater

1949 Ford V-8 'Pilot'

The British Ford Motor Co. brought out its first V-8 model, the '18F' of 3,622cc, in 1932. Following this came the V-8 II models, the '48F' (1935-36), the '68F' (1935-36) and the '78F' (1937-38). In 1938 the first V-8 III model appeared, the '81A', and in 1939 the '91A' with hydraulic brakes. Throughout this series the same 3½-litre engine was used, progressively modified and improved. Also Fords brought out a smaller V-8 model, of 2,227cc in 1935 and continued manufacture of this model until 1941. During the War these V-8 models became staff cars, giving excellent service, and when in 1947 the V-8 'Pilot' finally emerged, it still seemed reminiscent of a World War II staff car. Perhaps its mere 20 mpg during times of strict petrol rationing heralded its inevitable doom; nevertheless it remains an impressive and sought-after car to-day. One of its more exciting aspects was the manual gearbox, which afforded the thrill of extracting the maximum acceleration from its powerful engine. The body and chassis were built on a very robust scale, with large wings and a wide, capacious interior. Unusual mechanical aspects were its twin-contact-breaker distributor and the reliance on a six-volt electrical system, necessitating a powerful battery to supply current for starting. All accessories, (carburetter, generator, control-box, starter-motor, etc.) were of Ford pattern. Steering was of worm-and-roller type, suspension by transverse leaf-springs front and rear (rather antiquated), and brakes hydromechanical. A spiral bevel rear axle was fitted.

Features: Ex-WD reconditioned engines and other mechanical spares still obtainable (details below.) Body and chassis very solid. De-coke easy due to sv layout. Smooth, sprightly performance.

Failings: Ford Motor Co. probably doesn't bother to acknowledge this car now as regards spares. Rather high fuel consumption. Tyres scarce. Six-volt electrics inadequate for a 3½-litre engine. Exclusively 'Ford' parts (e.g. twin water pumps) do not always have substitutes. Hydromechanical brakes rather poor considering power and weight of car. Eight cylinders to overhaul if engine is worn.

Car Club Honorary Secretary: J.H. Bowkett, Glenhaven, Poundfield Way, Cookham, Berks.

SPARES: 1. (Ex-WD reconditioned engines and mechanical spares:) M. J. R. Knapman, 46 Morland Road, E. Croydon, Surrey (01-654 4969).
   2. (Plugs, gaskets, bearings:) Through Ford Spares stockists.
   3. (Carburetter:) If worn, replace with large 'Solex' downdraught type, or USA Carter.
   4. Through above club.

Ford V-8 'Pilot'

Engine (Mechanical)		Carburetter	
No. of cylinders : capacity	8; 3,622 cc	Original make	Ford
Bore and stroke	77·8 x 95·2 mm	Original type	Downdraught
Compression ratio	6·15 : 1	Choke tube	25
Valve layout	Side	Main jet	110
Tappet clearances	0·011–0·013 in. (cold)	Compensating jet	200
Location of valve timing marks	On camshaft and crankshaft gears	Pilot jet	55
		Auxiliary Air Bleed	80
Timing : inlet valve opens	9° 22' btdc	Starter Petrol jet	145
Piston withdrawal direction	Upwards	Starter Air jet	5·5
		Progression jet	60
Engine (Ignition)			
Firing order	1, 5, 4, 8, 6, 3, 7, 2	*Electrical Accessories*	
Location of timing marks	Distributor driving offset dog	Battery	6v 86 ah
		Original (Lucas) generator	Ford 2-brush
Timing : points open	—	Original (Lucas) control box	Ford
Original spark plugs	Champion C7	Original (Lucas) starter motor	Ford
Plug gap	0·025 in.		
Original (Lucas) coil	Ford		
Original (Lucas) distributor	Ford		

Chassis Components and Steering Geometry	
Brakes	Ford-Girling hydromechanical
Rear axle : Type	Spiral bevel
Ratio	4·11 : 1 (later 3·78 : 1)
Crown-wheel tooth contact	Adjustable by gaskets or adjusting nuts
Front suspension	Transverse leaf-spring
Rear suspension	Transverse leaf-spring
Steering pattern	Worm and roller
Toe-in	$\frac{1}{16} - \frac{1}{8}$ in.
Castor angle	4½–9°
Camber angle	3° 15' – 1° 7'
King-pin inclination	8° 9'

Lubrication	
Engine : Original S.A.E. grade	Summer 30, Winter 20
Quantity	8½ pt. including filter
Gearbox : Original S.A.E. grade	90 EP
Quantity	2 pt.
Rear axle : Original S.A.E. grade	90 EP
Quantity	2 pt.
Steering box : Original S.A.E. grade	90 EP

Tyres	
Size	6·50 x 16
Pressures (lb/in^2)	F : 25 R : 26-30

Healey 'Sportsmobile'

1949-50. 2½-litre Sports Roadster. 4 seater

Designed by a team led by Donald Healey, the 'Sportsmobile' utilized a 2½-litre Riley engine-and-gearbox unit of the RMB 1 series, fitted into an elongated, but otherwise standard, Healey chassis. The aim of the design was to provide comfortable seating for four passengers in an open sports car capable of travelling at 100 mile/h. In order to reduce the total weight, an aluminium body was employed. In overall style the 'Sportsmobile' typified the trends of the time, but broke away from the graceful style of earlier Healeys to incorporate streamlining in a more 'blocked-in' shape. All body panels were integral, with headlamps, radiator grille and

1949 Healey 'Sportsmobile'

wings blended into a single unit form. But somehow the result was still ungainly, the desire for 'unity', for example, producing identical flattened-off wheel openings in both front and rear wings. The engine, of four-cylinder in-line ohv pattern and 2,443cc capacity, developed 104 bhp at 4,500 rev/min, giving a top speed of 105 mile/h. A Riley 'torque tube' transmission shaft was employed, the majority of 'rear-end' mechancial components also being of Riley manufacture. Suspension pattern was independent coil front, and coil rear; brakes fully hydraulic. The 'Sportsmobile' suffered from a poor steering-mechanism design which incorporated a large triangular aluminium plate pivoted to the underside of the front chassis, and acting as a compensator in place of the usual idler fitted to most steering-box systems. The problem was that even the slightest wear in the pivot bearing resulted in wobble in the swivel plate and hence 'sloppy' steering. A very short-lived model, only 23 'Sportsmobiles' were ever built.

Features: Riley engine spares easy to obtain through Riley specialists. Aluminium bodywork very resistant to corrosion. Extremely comfortable interior. Excellent performance. The rarity of this model makes it very sought-after.
Failings: Body spares non-existent. Steering-gear a definite weak spot, demanding regular maintenance (club specialists will advise here).

Healey '3-Litre'

1951-52. Sports Convertible. 3 seater

This model, produced by the then still independent Donald Healey Motor Company, was an 'Anglicized' version of the Nash-Healey 'Sports Convertible' with its 3.8 litre Nash 'Dual Jetfire' six-cylinder engine replaced by an Alvis engine and gearbox. The 2,993cc Alvis engine developed 106 bhp at 4,200 rev/min and gave the 'Sports Convertible' a top speed of 100 mile/h. The original Nash-Healey model had been produced expressly for the USA market. An untypical radiator grille, to replace the Nash grille, was fitted into the oval air-intake (the Nash grille had fitted over the intake) but apart from that the design was pure 'Healey', and reminiscent of the prototype Healey '100'. Very forward-looking in concept, the body design incorporated an integral front- and rear-wing form, with the bonnet fully blended into the wings and front apron; headlamps, too, were integral with the front wings. A flat-paned two-piece 'V' windscreen was featured, together with a three-abreast single 'bench' seat. A strongly-constructed chassis was incorporated, with pressed steel bodywork and disc wheels. The brakes were fully hydraulic and suspension was of coil pattern on all four wheels. Marles steering gear was fitted. Regrettably, only 25 of these cars were built. (From 1952, Nash-Healeys had Farina styling and a 4.1-litre engine.)

Features: Very good performance. Alvis engine superbly built; Healey bodywork rugged and long-lasting. A very rare, sought-after model.

Failings: Engine spares will certainly be costly. Steel bodywork and chassis prone to corrosion. Rarity of model makes re-building in UK an extremely worthwhile, but onerous task. (404 Nash-Healeys built; USA enthusiasts may find it easier.)

Car Club Honorary Secretary: (Healey Register of Austin-Healey Club) I. Picton-Robinson, 12 Boxnott Close, Webheath, Redditch, Worcs.

SPARES: 1. ('Sportsmobile' engine:) see Riley section.
           2. ('3-Litre' engine:) see Alvis section.
           3. Through Jonathan Bowers, Austin-Healey Club.

	Healey 2·4-Litre 'Sportsmobile'	Healey '3-Litre' Sports Convertible (Alvis engine)
Engine (Mechanical)		
No. of cylinders : capacity	4; 2,443 cc	6; 2,993 cc
Bore and stroke	80·5 x 120 mm	84 x 90 mm
Compression ratio	6·89 : 1	7 : 1
Valve layout	Overhead	Overhead
Tappet clearances	Inlet 0·003 in. Exhaust 0.004 in. (hot)	Inlet 0·012 in. Exhaust 0·015 in. (hot)
Location of valve timing marks	On camshaft sprockets	On flywheel
Timing : inlet valve opens	17° btdc	13° btdc
Piston withdrawal direction	Upwards	Upwards
Engine (Ignition)		
Firing order	1, 2, 4, 3	1, 5, 3, 6, 2, 4
Location of timing marks	None	On flywheel
Timing : points open	4° btdc	2° btdc
Original spark plugs	Lodge HLNP	Champion L10
Plug gap	0·025 in.	0·025 in.
Original (Lucas) coil	B12	B12
Original (Lucas) distributor	DKY4A	DVXH-6A
Carburetters		
Original make	2 SU	2 SU
Original type	HV4	H4
Choke tube	–	–
Metering needle	AM	ES
Jet size	0·090	0·090
Electrical Accessories		
Battery	2 x 6v 63 ah	2 x 6v 63 ah
Original (Lucas) generator	–	C45PV
Original (Lucas) control box	–	RF95/2
Original (Lucas) starter motor	–	–
Chassis Components and Steering Geometry		
Brakes	Lockheed hydraulic	Girling hydraulic
Rear axle : Type	Spiral bevel (torque tube)	Hypoid bevel
Ratio	3·5 : 1	3·77 : 1
Crown-wheel tooth contact	Not adjustable	Not adjustable
Front suspension	Independent coil	Independent coil
Rear suspension	Coil	Coil
Steering Pattern	Bishop cam	Marles
Toe-in	1/8 – 1/4 in.	3/16 in.
Castor angle	0°	0–1°
Camber angle	0–1°	0–1°
King-pin inclination	9°	9°

1951 Healey '3-Litre'

	Healey 2·4-Litre 'Sportsmobile'	Healey '3-Litre' Sports Convertible (Alvis engine)
Lubrication		
Engine : Original S.A.E. grade	30	Summer 30, Winter 20
Quantity	12 pt.	12 pt.
Gearbox : Original S.A.E. grade	140 EP	30
Quantity	2 pt.	3 pt.
Rear axle : Original S.A.E. grade	140 EP	90 HYP
Quantity	5 pt.	3 pt.
Steering box : Original S.A.E. grade	140 EP	140 EP
Tyres		
Size	5·75 x 15	5·75 x 15 or 5·90 x 15
Pressures (lb/in^2)	F : 24 R : 24	F : 24 R : 24

HRG '1100' and '1500'

1946-55. 1- and 1½-litre Sports. 2 seater

In concept, the HRG combined rugged simplicity with a traditionally pre-war approach, and was intended to be suitable for both everyday open-air motoring and high-performance competition work. Production of the HRG began in 1935, and successes in both racing and trials events were achieved regularly each season both before, and after, the war. Virtually identical in outward appearance these post-war models were fitted with ohc engines of either 1,074cc or 1,496cc capacity, built largely from Singer components. The smaller unit, of 7.75 to 1 compression ratio, produced 44 bhp at 5,200 rev/min, giving a top speed in the 70s, while the larger, of 7 to 1 compression ratio, developed 61 bhp at 4,800 rev/min, giving a top speed of 90 mile/h. The aforementioned performance figures were with completely standard engines; high-compression pistons, a Scintilla 'Vertex' magneto and special gear ratios were offered as extras and these markedly stepped-up the performance and top speeds of both models. The carburation of both engines was by twin inclined SU carburetters, exhaust gas flow being little hindered in the fitting of a swept

1948 HRG '1500'

four-branch exhaust manifold. The body design changed little through the years – a long bonnet, open front mudguards, separate chromed headlamps, chromium-plated radiator shell, 'cut-away' doors and 'knock-on' wire wheels being characteristic features. The chassis frame was constructed of deep channel section, with tubular cross-bracing, and was light yet extremely sturdy. The front axle was in one piece and tubular, its suspension being provided by quarter-elliptic leaf springs and radius arms; the rear suspension was also of the traditional leaf spring type. A four-speed gearbox with central gear lever, and a spiral-bevel rear axle were fitted. Standard brakes were of the well-tried fully mechanical pattern, operated by cables and also individually adjustable, a master adjustment being mounted in the cockpit. The Electron alloy brake drums were of large diameter with central cooling fins and Centricast iron liners. Fully hydraulic brakes were an optional extra. Friction shockabsorbers were retained for the front suspension, while the rear wheels were served by both friction and hydraulic types. Steering was of Marles pattern. The cockpit itself had two adjustable bucket-type seats and luggage could be stowed behind these. The hood could be folded away beneath a tonneau cover and the windscreen could be locked at any angle or folded flat. Twin spare-wheel fittings for trials work were also offered as extras. The high performance of both engines was coupled with modest petrol consumption: 35-40 mpg for the 1,074cc unit and 30-33 mpg for the 1½-litre.

Features: A sports and competition car that provides a reminder of the flavour of pre-war high-performance motoring. A very rare and sought-after marque.
Failings: Scarcity of spares.

Car Club Honorary Secretary: I. Dussek, Hustyn, Packhorse Road, Bessels Green, Sevenoaks, Kent.
(Singer Owner's Club: D. Freeth, 31 Rivers Hill, Watton-at-Stone, Herts.)

SPARES: Major engine components obtainable through breakage of postwar Singer 'Nine' of 1946-52. Other parts (bodywork, etc.) virtually non-existent, except through above club.

	H.R.G. '1100'	H.R.G. '1500'
Engine (Mechanical)		
No. of cylinders : capacity	4; 1,074 cc	4; 1,496 cc
Bore and stroke	60 x 95 mm	68 x 103 mm
Compression ratio	7.75 : 1 or various	7 : 1 or various
Valve layout	ohc	ohc
Tappet clearances	Inlet 0·005 in. Exhaust 0·007 in.	Inlet 0·004 in. Exhaust 0·006 in.
Location of valve timing marks	On flywheel	On flywheel
Timing : inlet valve opens	20° btdc	5° btdc
Piston withdrawal direction	Downwards	Downwards

	H.R.G. '1100'	H.R.G. '1500'
Engine (Ignition)		
Firing order	1, 3, 4, 2	1, 3, 4, 2
Location of timing marks	1—4 on flywheel	1—4 on flywheel
Timing : points open	—	—
Original spark plugs	Champion L10S	Champion L10S
Plug gap	0·025—0·030 in.	0·025—0·030 in.
Original (Lucas) coil	Q12 or Scintilla magneto	Q12 or Scintilla magneto
Original (Lucas) distributor	DK4A	DK4A
Carburetters		
Original make	2 SU	2 SU
Original type	Semi-downdraught	Semi-downdraught
Electrical Accessories		
Battery	12v 50 ah	12v 50 ah
Original (Lucas) generator	C45YV	C45YV
Original (Lucas) control box	RF91	RF95/2
Original (Lucas) starter motor	M35G/L	M35G/L
Chassis Components		
Brakes	Girling mechanical or hydraulic	Girling mechanical or hydraulic
Rear axle : Type	Spiral bevel	Spiral bevel
Ratio	4·55 : 1 or various	4 : 1 or various
Crown-wheel tooth contact	Adjustable by shims	Adjustable by shims
Front suspension	Quarter-elliptic and radius arms	Quarter-elliptic and radius arms
Rear suspension	Semi-elliptic	Semi-elliptic
Steering Pattern	Marles Adamant	Marles Adamant
Lubrication		
Engine : Original S.A.E. grade	30	30
Quantity	7 pt.	11 pt.
Gearbox : Original S.A.E. grade	40	40
Quantity	2 pt.	2¾ pt.
Rear axle : Original S.A.E. grade	90 EP	140 EP
Quantity	2 pt.	3 pt.
Steering box : Original S.A.E. grade	90 EP	140 EP
Tyres		
Size	5·50 x 16	5·50 x 16

Jaguar 'XK 120'

1949-54. 3½-litre Super Sports Roadster. 2 seater

The pre-war SS Cars Ltd became Jaguar Cars Ltd in 1945. At that time the design team comprised William Lyons, William Heynes, Walter Hassan and Claude Baily as chief designer. This team set about producing a smooth, flexible engine of high power output and capable of continuous development, to supercede the performance of the engine used in the 1936 SS Jaguar 100. Their goal was to develop a unit capable of producing 160 bhp, to be used to power their projected 'Mk VII' saloon. Four-cylinder engines, coded XF and XG came first, then the XJ units of four-cylinder two litre and six-cylinder 3.2 litre type. Due to inadequate low-speed torque the stroke of the XJ 'six' was increased to give a capacity of 3,442cc, and this became the XK engine. Earls Court, 1948, saw the first appearance of a prototype two-seater called the 'XK 100'; it was a beautiful body design by William Lyons powered by a four-cylinder two-litre XJ engine. But the 'XK 100' never went into production, for by 1949 the 3½ litre XK engine was

1950 Jaguar 'XK 120' Roadster

1951 Jaguar 'XK 120' Fixed-head Coupé

found to be far superior — and so the 'XK 120' Roadster was born. The dohc XK engine developed 162 bhp at 5,200 rev/min, the '120' standing for the maximum speed. Carburation was by twin SU carburetters. The body shape had large, bulky front wings, the lines of which stretched back to 'butt-joint' against the rear wings at a point coinciding with the rear edge of the doors. The curving bonnet tapered outwards rapidly towards the windscreen from a diminutive, upright-oval radiator grille. A very brief divided front bumper was fitted, and the headlamps and sidelights were blended into the front wings. The high curving line of the bonnet continued in a descending arc across the rear and boot. Solid pressed-steel wheels were fitted. (By today's standards the design might be considered too bulky and front-heavy.) The sturdy box-sectioned chassis had X-bracing to ensure torsional rigidity; suspension was by torsion-bars for the front wheels and leaf-springs for the rear. Steering was of Burman recirculating ball pattern; brakes were fully hydraulic with 12in. drums (and were, in fact, inadequate for high speed driving). The 'XK 120' had the traditional Moss gearbox. Jaguars originally intended to produce only 200 'XK 120' models, but due to public demand a full production programme had to be laid down. These first 200 models had aluminium bodies, mounted on a wooden frame. Fastest speed recorded by an 'XK 120' was 172 mile/h, the model being a stripped Roadster with modified engine, incorporating a perspex dome over the cockpit.

Features: Engine superbly built. Rugged chassis, solid bodywork. Exciting performance together with comfort. Interior very well appointed.
Failings: Engine has tendency to overheat (fit 'Kenlowe' fan). Tired thermostatic choke over-richens mixture (remedy: fit manual choke). Brakes poor considering weight and performance. Chassis demands constant maintenance, (and bodywork if steel). Wooden-framed bodies need checking for rot. Gearbox is notoriously slow-changing. Spares expensive and very scarce.

Jaguar 'Mk VII'

1950-54. 3½-litre Sports Saloon. 5-6 seater

The 'XK 120' engine was fitted also in the 'Mk VII' of 1950. Contrasting with the earlier 'Mk V', full streamlining was employed in the body design, a virtual compromise between the 'Mk V' and the 'XK'. The bulky front wings, blended headlamps, and falling curve of the boot were combined with a smaller, still semi-traditional radiator grille, the rear window and adjacent roof area being virtually unchanged from earlier saloons. Top speed of the 'Mk VII' was 106 mile/h. The bodywork was of steel and the chassis of 'XK' pattern: rugged box-section with X-bracing. A Moss four-speed gearbox was fitted, operated by a floor-mounted gear lever. Suspension was by torsion-bars for the front wheels and leaf-springs for the rear. Brakes were fully hydraulic, servo-assisted. Laycock-De Normanville overdrive was an optional extra. Interior finish was excellent, hide upholstery being used together with walnut for the fascia and door cappings.

Features: Engine identical to 'XK 120'. Very solidly built. Excellent performance with luxury-car comfort.

1951 Jaguar 'Mk VII'

Failings: Chassis and bodywork need constant maintenance, particularly box-like shelf under front wings (remedy: drill ½in. drain holes). Moss gearbox sluggish. Exhaust system large, complicated and costly to replace. As with 'XK', tyres are expensive and difficult to trace. All spares expensive and now scarce.

Car Club Honorary Secretary: Mrs. M. Wheeler, Norfolk Hotel, Harrington Road, South Kensington.
(XK Club:) Bob Hadfield, 103 Belvoir Street, Hull, Yorks.
(XK Register:) Ron Bradshaw, 41 Ingrave Rd, Brentwood, Essex.

SPARES: 1. Jaguar agents, but to a very limited degree.
2. (XK 120:) Berkswell (Warwicks.) 3484.
3. (XK 120 and Mk. VII repairs:) Townley Road Garage, Bexleyheath, Kent (01-304 4589).
4. Through above clubs.

	Jaguar 'XK 120' Roadster	Jaguar 'Mk VII'
Engine (Mechanical)		
No. of cylinders : capacity	6; 3,442 cc	6; 3,442 cc
Bore and stroke	83 x 106 mm	83 x 106 mm
Compression ratio	7 or 8 : 1	7 or 8 : 1
Valve layout	Overhead (twin ohc)	Overhead (twin ohc)
Tappet clearances	Inlet 0·004 in. Exhaust 0·006 in.	Inlet 0·004 in. Exhaust 0·006 in.
Location of valve timing marks	On flywheel and front camshaft journals	On flywheel and front camshaft journals
Timing : inlet valve opens	15° btdc	10–15° btdc
Piston withdrawal direction	Upwards, with con. rod	Upwards, with con. rod
Engine (Ignition)		
Firing order	1, 5, 3, 6, 2, 4	1, 5, 3, 6, 2, 4
Location of timing marks	On flywheel and crankcase	On flywheel and crankcase
Timing : points open	5° btdc	7 : 1 – tdc
		8 : 1 – 5° btdc
Original spark plugs	7 : 1 – Champion L1OS	7 : 1 – Champion L1OS
	8 : 1 – Champion N8B	8 : 1 – Champion N8B
Plug gap	0·022 in.	0·022 in.
Original (Lucas) coil	B12	B12 or HA12
Original (Lucas) distributor	7 : 1 – GC50	GC50/53 or DVX6A
	8 : 1 – GC53	
Carburetters		
Original make	2 SU	2 SU
Original type	H6	H6
Metering needle	RF	SM or SR
Jet size	0·100 in.	0·100 in.
Electrical Accessories		
Battery	12v 63 ah	12v 63 ah
Original (Lucas) generator	C45PV/S	C45PV/S
Original (Lucas) control box	RB106/1	RB106/1
Original (Lucas) starter motor	M45G	M45G

1951 Jaguar 'Mk VII' dashboard

	Jaguar 'XK 120' Roadster	Jaguar 'Mk VII'
Chassis Components and Steering Geometry		
Brakes	Lockheed hydraulic	Girling vac. servo
Rear axle : Type	Hypoid bevel	Hypoid bevel
Ratio	Various	4·27 : 1 (overdrive 4·55 : 1)
Crown-wheel tooth contact	Adjustable	Adjustable
Front suspension	Torsion bars	Torsion bars
Rear suspension	Semi-elliptic leaf	Semi-elliptic leaf
Steering pattern	Recirculating ball	Recirculating ball
Toe-in	$1/8 - 3/16$ in.	$1/8 - 3/16$ in.
Castor angle	$5°$ (later $3°$)	$1/4°$ neg. — $1/4°$ pos.
Camber angle	$1¾-2°$	$1°$ positive
King-pin inclination	$5°$	$8°$
Lubrication		
Engine : Original S.A.E. grade	Summer 30, Winter 20	Summer 30, Winter 20
Quantity	Sump: 24 pt.	Sump: 19 or 21 pt.
	Total: 29 pt.	Total: 22 or 24 pt.
Gearbox : Original S.A.E. grade	30	30
Quantity	2½ pt.	2½ pt. (overdrive 4 pt.)
Rear axle : Original S.A.E. grade	90 HYP	90 HYP
Quantity	3½ pt.	3½ pt.
Steering box : Original S.A.E. grade	140 EP	140 EP
Tyres		
Size	6·00 x 16	6·70 x 16
Pressures (lb/in^2)	F : 25 R : 25	F : 23 R : 25

Jensen 'Interceptor'

1951-56. 4-litre Convertible. 5-6 seater

1951 Jensen 'Interceptor' Convertible

The aim of Jensen Motors in designing the 'Interceptor' was to provide a car with a sizeable engine and high gearing; this resulted in a fast crusing speed at low engine speed coupled with effortless, silent performance and longevity for the engine. To power this model Jensens chose an Austin A.125 'Sheerline' engine of 3,993cc, developing 130 bhp at 3,700 rev/min. Due to the aluminium body fitted, which considerably reduced the total weight of the car, top speed was approximately 100 mile/h, 70 mile/h being attainable in third gear. A four-speed gearbox plus overdrive was fitted, fuel consumption being 20-24 mpg. In appearance the 'Interceptor' was far from old-fashioned; full width frontal aspect being employed, an oval air-intake set low down, and an integral form coupling together both the front and rear wings, the door panels being cut out of this single homogenous shape. Headlamps were integral, too, with the front wings and bonnet; massive chromed bumpers were fitted at front and rear, and disc wheels. A sturdy steel chassis was essential in anchoring the lightweight body, and brakes were fully hydraulic; suspension pattern was of independent coil-and-wishbone for the front wheels, with leaf-springs for the rear. A hypoid rear axle of 3.77 to 1 ratio was fitted, overdrive reducing this ratio in top gear to 2.85 to 1 — hence the low piston speed of 2,500 ft/min at 97 mile/h, ensuring long engine life free of major overhauls.

Features: A large, comfortable, fast and silent car. The 4-litre engine will give very long service, Austin spares do not pose an insurmountable problem as yet. Alloy bodywork can last indefinitely, if maintained. Fuel consumption of this large-capacity engine, whilst acceptable when in good condition, can drop to 12-15 mpg when worn.

Failings: Body spares and interior fittings virtually unobtainable now.

1951 Jensen 'Interceptor' Fixed-head Coupé

Jensen '541'

1955-56. 4-litre Sports Saloon. 2/4 seater

The '541' followed the 'Interceptor', employing the same engine with a few modifications, *i.e.* choice of a higher compression ratio (6.8 or 7.4 to 1). The greatest innovation was the body fabric, the chosen material for which was fibreglass, thus taking advantage of its high strength/weight ratio; also corrosion problems were non-existent with this material. The design of the body was typical of the trends at that time: fully integral bonnet, grille and wings, and a 'fastback', Jensens by this time favouring the hard-top formula. Due to the fibreglass body, a sturdy chassis was essential to the structure of the car. In 1955, the 'standard' engine, still developing 130 bhp at the surprisingly low figure of 3,700 rev/min, gave a top speed of 105 mile/h. The low engine speed at peak power necessitated the fitting of a rear axle of very high ratio (2.93 to 1) on models without overdrive, but this again was a deliberate feature of the design, parallel to the 'Interceptor' with its fast cruising speed and leisurely engine revs. The brakes of the '541' were fully hydraulic and servo-assisted; suspension pattern was independent coil for the front wheels, with traditional leaf-springs retained for the rear. (In 1956 the 'De Luxe' version appeared, and in 1957 the high-speed 'R' series powered by an Austin DS7 engine.)

Features: Austin spares for the engine. Very efficient brakes. Exterior finely finished and interior very well appointed. True chassis fitted: Fibreglass body will not corrode — repairs are simple D.I.Y.

Failings: Rather high fuel consumption. Body fittings, etc. rare and costly (perhaps unobtainable now).

Car Club Honorary Secretary: L. Jackson, 40 Station Rd, St. Margarets, Ware, Herts.

SPARES: 1. Perhaps through vintage Austin specialists, for engine parts.
2. 'Cannibalization' from engine of wrecked Austin A.125 'Sheerline'.
3. Bodywork repairs ('541'): use fibreglass cloth, polyester resin and paste.

1955 Jensen '541'

	Jensen 'Interceptor'	Jensen '541'
Engine (Mechanical)		
No. of cylinders : capacity	6; 3,993 cc	6; 3,993 cc
Bore and stroke	87 x 111 mm	87 x 111 mm
Compression ratio	6·8 : 1	6·8 or 7·4 : 1
Valve layout	Overhead	Overhead
Tappet clearances	0·012 in.	0·012 in.
Location of valve timing marks	Spots on gears	Spots on gears
Timing : inlet valve opens	5° btdc	5° btdc
Piston withdrawal direction	Upwards	Upwards
Engine (Ignition)		
Firing order	1, 5, 3, 6, 2, 4	1, 5, 3, 6, 2, 4
Location of timing marks	tdc 1 on flywheel	tdc 1 on flywheel
Timing : points open	tdc	tdc
Original spark plugs	Champion N8B	Champion N8B
Plug gap	0·035 in.	0·035 in.
Original (Lucas) coil	B12	B12
Original (Lucas) distributor	DX6A/BN172	DX6A/BN172
Carburetters		
Original make	Stromberg	S U
Original type	—	H4
Choke tube	1³/₈ in.	Metering needle CZ
Main jet	0.063	—
By-pass Jet	0·046	—
Electrical Accessories		
Battery	12v 64 ah	12v 64 ah
Original (Lucas) generator	C45PV/45	C45PV/45
Original (Lucas) control box	RB310	RB310
Original (Lucas) starter motor	M45G	M45G
Chassis Components and Steering Geometry		
Brakes	Girling hydraulic	Girling hydraulic, servo-assisted
Rear axle : Type	Hypoid bevel	Hypoid bevel
Ratio	3·77 : 1	2·93 : 1
Crown-wheel tooth contact	Not adjustable	Not adjustable
Front suspension	Independent coil	Independent coil
Rear suspension	Semi-elliptic leaf	Semi-elliptic leaf
Steering pattern	Cam and sector	Cam and sector
Toe-in	¹/₁₆ in.	¹/₁₆ in.
Castor angle	1¼°	2°
Camber angle	1°	½°
King-pin inclination	6½°	6¾°
Lubrication		
Engine : Original S.A.E. grade	Summer 30, Winter 20	Summer 30, Winter 20
Quantity	17 pt. inc. filter	17 pt. inc. filter
Gearbox : Original S.A.E. grade	30	30
Quantity	8 pt.	6½ pt. (overdrive 8 pt.)
Rear axle : Original S.A. E. grade	90 HYP	90 HYP
Quantity	4 pt.	3 pt.
Steering box : Original S.A.E. grade	90 EP	90 EP
Tyres		
Size	6·00 x 16	6·00 x 16
Pressures (lb/in²)	F : 28 R : 28	F : 28 R : 28

Jowett 'Javelin'

PA, PB, PC, PD, PE. 1947-54. 1½-litre Saloon. 4-5 seater

The designer, Gerald Palmer, began work on the prototype Javelin in 1942. Rumour has it that he based the design on either the Lancia 'Aprilia' or the V-12 Lincoln 'Zephyr'. The finalized production model appeared in 1947, and featured a 'flat-four' engine design, *i.e.* with pairs of cylinders horizontally opposed. A further feature of the engine was an all-aluminium block with wet cylinder liners. The early 'PA' engine produced 50 bhp at 4,100 rev/min, giving a top speed of 78 mile/h. This was on postwar 'Pool' petrol of 76-80 Octane, fuel consumption being 28-30 mpg. The compression ratio of the engine was 7.2 to 1. One of its major failings was the crankshaft, which often broke because of metal fatigue. This was corrected in later models by fitting a more massive drilled-web design, the webs being deliberately left un-machined, and shot-peened after casting. The engine of the final 'PE' model developed 52.5 bhp at 4,500 rev/min, giving a top speed in 1954 of 82 mile/h. In appearance, the 'Javelin' had an aerodynamic body design with full streamlining of the bonnet, wings, roof, and rear. The radiator grille was of an inverted-T shape, broad at the base to ensure cooling of the front brake drums and low-positioned engine. Headlamps and sidelights were integral with the front wings, and the curves of the bonnet and wings swept back in a 'high prow' layout to the curving, high roof and the characteristic 'Javelin fastback'. Bodywork was in pressed steel, and the chassis of box-section type. Brakes of the 'PA' and 'PB' were hydromechanical; later models were fully hydraulic. Suspension pattern on all models was of torsion bars on all four wheels; a four-speed gearbox was fitted, operated by a column-mounted gear lever. Due to low engine positioning, all postwar Jowetts had a completely flat floor, the entire seating plan lying within the wheelbase. There was a choice of 'standard' or 'de luxe' interiors. The Jowett Car Co. was liquidated in 1954.

Features: Flat-four engine gives long service; twin carburetters fitted; alloy block makes engine removal easy. Radiator is at rear of engine, giving excellent accessibility to contact-breaker, etc. 'Layrub' couplings in transmission give very smooth power transfer. Very keen Car Club. Spares still readily available (see addresses below).

Failings: Low power/weight ratio. Steel bodywork and box-section chassis very prone to corrosion. Rather cramped engine compartment for certain operations, despite rear radiator. Engines tend to run cool. Gearboxes tend to leak. 'PA' and 'PB' engines have hydraulic tappets.

1951 Jowett 'Javelin'

	Jowett 'Javelin' PA, PB, PC, PD, PE	Jowett 'Jupiter' SA, SC
Engine (Mechanical)		
No. of cylinders : capacity	4; 1,486 cc	4; 1,486 cc
Bore and stroke	72·5 x 90 mm	72·5 x 90 mm
Compression ratio	7·2 : 1	8 : 1
Valve layout	Overhead	Overhead

Tappet clearances	PA, PB : Inlet 0·060 in.
	       Exhaust 0·090 in. (dry)
	PC, PD, PE : Inlet 0·002 in.
	       Exhaust 0·006 in. (cold)
		Inlet 0.002-0.004 in. Exhaust
		0.006-0.008 in. (cold)

Location of valve timing marks	On flywheel	On flywheel
Timing : inlet valve opens	PA, PB, PC : tdc PD, PE : 12° btdc	12° btdc
Piston withdrawal direction	Remove liner upwards	Remove liner upwards

	Jowett 'Javelin' PA, PB, PC, PD, PE		Jowett 'Jupiter' SA, SC	
Engine (Ignition)				
Firing order	1, 4, 2, 3		1, 4, 2, 3	
Location of timing marks	On flywheel		On flywheel	
Timing : points open	tdc to $^3/_8$ in. atdc		tdc to $^3/_8$ in. atdc	
Original spark plugs	Champion L10		Champion L10S	
Plug gap	0·020—0·025 in.		0·020—0·025 in.	
Original (Lucas) coil	Q12		Q12	
Original (Lucas) distributer	DKYH4A/DM2		DKYH4A/DM2	
Carburetters				
Original make	Zenith		Zenith	
Original type	30 VM5 (PA: VM4)		30 VIG5 or 30 VM	
Choke tube	23		26	27
Main jet	90		105	120
Compensating jet	50		60	65
Slow-running jet	45		45	45
Progression jet	110		—	120
Pump jet	—		90	—
Electrical Accessories				
Battery	12v 50 ah		2 x 6v 50 ah	
Original (Lucas) generator	C39 (PA: C45)		C45PV/4	
Original (Lucas) control box	RF95/2		RF95 (later RB106)	
Original (Lucas) starter motor	M35G		M35G	
Chassis Components and Steering Geometry				
Brakes	PA, PB : Girling hydromechanical PC, PD, PE : Girling hydraulic		Girling hydraulic	
Rear axle : Type	Hypoid bevel		Hypoid bevel	
Ratio	4·88 : 1		4·56 : 1	
Crown-wheel tooth contact	Adjustable by shims		Adjustable by shims	
Front suspension	Torsion bars and wishbones		Torsion bars and wishbones	
Rear suspension	Transverse torsion bars		Transverse torsion bars	
Steering pattern	Internal gear and pinion		Rack and pinion	
Toe-in	0—$^1/_8$ in.		0—$^1/_8$ in.	
Castor angle	1¼°		1¼°	
Camber angle	Nil		Nil	
King-pin inclination	10°		10°	
Lubrication				
Engine : Original S.A.E. grade	30		30	
Quantity	PA, PB, PC : 9 pt. PD, PE : 10pt.		10 pt.	
Gearbox : Original S.A.E. grade	30		30	
Quantity	1 pt.		1 pt.	
Rear axle : Original S.A.E. grade	90 HYP		90 HYP	
Quantity	PA, PB, PC : 2 pt. PD, PE : 2¼ pt.		2¼ pt.	
Steering box : Original S.A.E. grade	Medium grease		Medium grease	
Tyres				
Size	5·25 x 16		5·50 x 16	
Pressures (lb/in^2)	F : 26	R : 26	F : 21	R : 23

Jowett 'Jupiter'

SA, SC. 1949-54. 1½-litre Sports. 2-3 seater

1952 Jowett 'Jupiter', owned by the author

Designed by Robert Eberan von Eberhorst, famous for his design work on 1938-39 Auto Union racing cars, the 'Jupiter', while intended as a sports variant of the 'Javelin', was in fact far removed from a 'Javelin' coupe. It was a distinct design of its own — the two models, placed side by side, might have come from two different manufacturers — yet under the surface a great many of the mechanical parts were the same. The engine was 'Javelin' based, i.e. a 'flat four' of 1,486cc, but with a higher compression ratio, developing 60 bhp at 4,750 rev/min, and giving a top speed of over 90 mile/h. But the bodywork was in alloy and the chassis a tubular steel semi-space frame. There was a small upright-oval radiator grill, a curving bonnet-and-front-wings front section, the 'high prow' bonnet line sweeping rearwards to a very distinctive long, tapering back. Both the front and rear wings were wide and bulging; with the hood down, the whole effect was very graceful and aerodynamic. The brakes were fully hydraulic, suspension pattern again torsion bars all round, and the steering box was of the rack-and-pinion type. A four-speed 'column change' gearbox was fitted, together with a divided transmission shaft incorporating a 'Layrub' coupling, and a hypoid rear axle. The 'SA' had an internal 'box' boot; the 'SC' had a boot lid, improved Series III engine and rubber-bushed front suspension. A total of only 1,000 'Jupiters' were built.

Features: Aluminium body, tubular steel chassis. Majority of mechanical parts identical to the more common 'Javelin'. Complete bonnet-and-wings section lifts to fully expose engine and front chassis. Steering very light and positive; centre of gravity very low.

Failings: Central body panel is pressed steel for rigidity, but very prone to corrosion. Large, empty bonnet gives engine noise echo.

Car Club Honorary Secretary: A.A.R. Pluckrose, The Briars, Castledon Road, Dowham, Billericay, Essex.

SPARES: 1. C. Moar, Rosehall Works, Shawhead, Coatbridge, Lanarks, Scotland.
2. G. Mitchell, Thrums, Cleish, Kinross, Scotland.
3. Through above club.

1952 Jowett 'Jupiter', owned by the author

Lagonda '2.6-Litre'

1949-53. 2½-litre Saloon. 6 seater

1951 Lagonda '2.6-Litre'

Designed by W.O. Bentley, the '2.6-Litre' replaced the prewar V-12. Shortly after the design-work was completed, in 1947, Lagonda was absorbed into the David Brown group to become Aston Martin Lagonda Ltd, and David Brown himself re-designed the prototype. (Shortly after this Tickfords, the car-body builders, were added to the combine.) The original Cotal gearbox was replaced by a David Brown synchromesh type, production commencing early in 1949, the Lagonda engine being retained. This unit was a six-cylinder dohc in-line design of 2,580cc, large-area thimble tappets being employed working direct on the cams, thus minimizing wear and eliminating the need for tappet adjustment. The valves were set at an included angle of 60º, the coolant contacting the exhaust valve guides direct. Detachable wet cylinder liners were used, the massive crankshaft had four bearings and the engine casing was in alloy. The engine developed 105 bhp at 5,000 rev/min, the compression ratio being 6.5 to 1. (No Mk 1 '2.6' had the higher-compression 'Vantage' engine fitted as original.) The body styling was forward-looking, with sweeping wings and an airflow shape, the traditional Lagonda radiator shell giving way to a curved grille following the line of the bonnet. The alloy bodywork was by Tickford, brakes were fully hydraulic and steering type was rack-and-pinion. Suspension was fully independent, with coils for the front wheels and torsion bars with De Dion axle for the rear. The car had a completely flat and low floor, the hypoid final drive and rear brake fixtures being mounted on the chassis; drive to the rear wheels was by open shafts via constant-velocity universal joints. The Mk II model appeared at the 1952 Motor Show with the 'Vantage' engine, but there were only very slight external differences. In all, a total of only 550 or so '2.6's were built.

Features: Alloy bodywork, robust chassis, remarkable Lagonda engine. 'Vantage' substitute engines step-up performance considerably. Alloy body panels should last indefinitely. Flat floor very convenient.
Failings: If needed, body parts will be very scarce. Column gear-change not as positive as floor-mounted type. Inaccessible mechanics at rear of chassis.

Lagonda '3-Litre'

1953-56. 3-litre Convertible. 4-5 seater

First appearing at the 1953 Motor Show, the new '3-Litre' used the '2.6' chassis, a bored-out '2.6' block and an alloy body of more modern form, built as before by Tickford. The engine was now of 2,922cc capacity, of 8.2 to 1 compression ratio, of dohc pattern as in the 2½-litre engine, and developed 140 bhp at 5,000 rev/min. Top speed was in the region of 110 mile/h. While still retaining the curved grille of the earlier model, the body design was far less 'undulating', the top line of the front wings sweeping rearwards through the door panels to merge imperceptibly with the upper line of the boot. The rear wings, too, were far less bold, emerging unobtrusively from the main integral body form. The headlamps were merged into the front wings and a large one-piece curving windscreen was fitted. Disc wheels were retained. Chassis specifications remained identical with the '2.6'; both used the same rear axle ratio of 4.56 to 1. In 1956 the convertible model was dropped, the Mk II saloon version appearing, fitted with a floor-mounted gearchange. In all a total of only 420 or so '3-Litres' were built. (The contemporary Aston Martin 'DB 2-4' used the same engine.)

Features: As for the '2.6-Litre', but with a higher performance and more timeless body design.

Failings: As for the '2.6-Litre'. Necessarily higher fuel consumption.

Car Club Honorary Secretary: Mrs. V.E. May, 68 Savill Rd, Lindfield, Haywards Heath, Sussex.

(USA representative:) R. T. Crane, 10 Crestwood Trail, Lake Mohawk, Sparta, NJ 07871.

SPARES: Through above club; Aston Martin Lagonda Ltd no longer able to assist.

1954 Lagonda '3-Litre'

	Lagonda '2·6-Litre'	Lagonda '3-Litre'
Engine (Mechanical)		
No. of cylinders : capacity	6; 2,580 cc	6; 2,922 cc
Bore and stroke	78 x 90 mm	83 x 90 mm
Compression ratio	6·5 : 1	8·2 : 1
Valve layout	twin ohc	twin ohc
Tappet clearances	Inlet 0·011—0·013 in.	Inlet 0·011—0·013 in.
	Exhaust 0·012—0·014 in.	Exhaust 0·012—0·014 in.
Location of valve timing marks	Crankshaft sprocket markings adjacent and in line	Crankshaft sprocket markings adjacent and in line
Timing : inlet valve opens	10° atdc	10° atdc
Piston withdrawal direction	Upwards	Upwards
Engine (Ignition)		
Firing order	1,5,3,6,2,4	1,5,3,6,2,4
Location of timing marks	tdc mark on flywheel	tdc mark on flywheel
Timing : points open	10° btdc retarded	10° btdc retarded
Original spark plugs	K.L.G. P10	K.L.G. L50
Plug gap	0·022 in.	0·022 in.
Original (Lucas) coil	B12-1	B12-1
Original (Lucas) distributor	DVXH6A	DVXH6A
Carburetters		
Original make	2 SU	2 SU
Original type	H4 or H6	H6
Choke tube	$1^5/_8$ in.	$1^3/_4$ in.
Metering needle	—	LB2
Electrical Accessories		
Battery	12v 51 ah	12 v 63 ah
Original (Lucas) generator	C45PVS/5	C45PVS/5
Original (Lucas) control box	RF95/2	RB106/2
Original (Lucas) starter motor	M45G	M45G
Chassis Components and Steering Geometry		
Brakes	Lockheed hydraulic	Lockheed hydraulic
Rear axle : Type	Hypoid bevel (De Dion)	Hypoid bevel (De Dion)
Ratio	4·56 : 1	4·56 : 1
Crown-wheel tooth contact	Adjustable by shims	Adjustable by shims
Front suspension	Independent coil	Independent coil
Rear suspension	Independent torsion bars	Independent torsion bars
Steering Pattern	Rack and pinion	Rack and pinion
Toe-in	$1/_8$ in.	$1/_8$ in.
Castor angle	2½°	2½°
Camber angle	1½°	1½°
King-pin inclination	5½°	5½°
Lubrication		
Engine : Original S.A.E. grade	Summer 40, Winter 30	Summer 40, Winter 30
Quantity	12 pt.	12 pt.
Gearbox : Original S.A.E. grade	90 EP	90 EP
Quantity	2¼ pt.	2¼ pt.
Rear axle : Original S.A.E. grade	90 HYP	90 HYP
Quantity	2 pt.	2 pt.
Steering box : Original S.A.E. grade	90 EP	90 EP
Tyres		
Size	6·00 x 16	6·00 x 16
Pressures (lb/in^2)	F : 25 R : 30	F : 25 R : 30

1954 Lagonda '3-Litre'

Lanchester 'LD10'

1946-51. 1¼-litre Saloon. 4-5 seater

1947 Lanchester 'LD 10' six-light Saloon

Lanchester was taken over by Daimler in 1931, hence from that time Lanchesters may be thought of as 'small Daimlers'. In 1946 the 'LD10' appeared — a smallish, very compact car with 4-cylinder in-line engine of 1,287cc capacity and 7 to 1 compression ratio. The six-light pressed steel body was built at first by Briggs, and they continued to manufacture this type of body until 1949, when it was replaced by a Barker four-light coach-built body. A chassis was incorporated in both designs. The six-light design was not particularly adventurous, being reminiscent of the 1938-39 Austin '10' in general form; front and rear wings exposed the wheels fully and it represented virtually a continuation of traditional prewar practice, even down to the separate chromed headlamps. The Barker body was certainly more graceful, and less like a taxi-cab, the four-light design providing a larger area of cellulose around the rear windows and a more flowing line around the boot and rear wings. Both types of 'LD10' retained the Lanchester pre-selector gearbox and fluid flywheel. One very unadventurous step was the retention of fully-mechanical brakes throughout.

Features: Coach-built body well made. True chassis incorporated. Reasonable fuel consumption.
Failings: New spares difficult and expensive. Body very prone to rusting. Mechanical brakes primitive for 1970s.

Lanchester 'LJ200' and 'LJ201'

1950-54. 2-litre Saloon. 4-5 seater

The 'Leda', produced for export, and the new '14' shared a completely revised chassis with larger engine of 1,968cc. The four-cylinder ohv pattern was retained, the compression ratio being lowered somewhat, maximum power being 60 bhp at 4,200 rev/min. Top speed was in the region of 75-80 mile/h. The body for the British market was again by Barker and in alloy, but this time a six-light design, with the headlamps blended into the front wings, which were more streamlined and their form elongated into the front door panels. Export versions had steel bodies. Revision of the prewar chassis was necessary to take the laminated torsion-bar suspension used on the front wheels; leaf-springs were retained for the rear. Girling hydromechanical brakes were fitted. The 'Leda' also employed a pre-selector gearbox in the Lanchester tradition, power being transmitted to the rear wheels via a worm drive to the hypoid axle. The Lanchester Company was dissolved in the late 1950s.

Features: Well-built Barker bodywork. Tyres still common — small rim size. Very smooth running and power transfer. (LJ201 chassis number indicates l h d model.)

Failings: New spares difficult to obtain and expensive. Export bodywork prone to severe rusting.

Car Club Honorary Secretary: Incorporated with Daimler Club.

SPARES: Through above club.

1951 Lanchester '14'

	Lanchester 'LD10' ('Ten')	Lanchester 'LJ200' and 'LJ201' ('Fourteen')
Engine (Mechanical)		
No. of cylinders : capacity	4; 1,287 cc	4; 1,968 cc
Bore and stroke	63·5 x 101·6 mm	76·2 x 107·9 mm
Compression ratio	7 : 1	6·7 : 1
Valve layout	Overhead	Overhead
Tappet clearances	0·012 in. (hot)	0·013 in. (hot)
Location of valve timing marks	Hole in camshaft chainwheel	Groove on flywheel
Timing : inlet valve opens	5° btdc	9° btdc
Piston withdrawal direction	Upwards, less con. rod	Upwards or downwards
Engine (Ignition)		
Firing order	1, 3, 4, 2	1, 3, 4, 2
Location of timing marks	On flywheel ring	On flywheel ring
Timing : points open	11° btdc	9° btdc
Original spark plugs	Lodge CB14	Lodge CLNH
Plug gap	0·030 in.	0·025 in.
Original (Lucas) coil	B12	B12
Original (Lucas) distributor	DVX4A	DM2
Carburetters		
Original make	Zenith	Zenith
Original type	VIG3	VIS36
Choke tube	23	27
Main jet	70	85
Compensating jet	80	85
Slow-running jet	50	60
Pump jet	50	50
Electrical Accessories		
Battery	12v 58 ah	12v 64 ah
Original (Lucas) generator	C45YV/3	C39PV/2
Original (Lucas) control box	RF95/2	RF106/1
Original (Lucas) starter motor	M35G	M418G

	Lanchester 'LD10' ('Ten')	Lanchester 'LJ200' and 'LJ201' ('Fourteen')
Chassis Components and Steering Geometry		
Brakes	Girling mechanical	Girling hydromechanical
Rear axle : Type	Spiral bevel	Hypoid bevel
Ratio	4·28 : 1	4·56 : 1
Crown-wheel tooth contact	Adjustable by shims	Adjustable by shims
Front suspension	Independent coil	Torsion bars
Rear suspension	Semi-elliptic leaf	Semi-elliptic leaf
Steering pattern	Cam and lever	Cam and lever
Toe-in	$1/_8$ in.	$1/_8$ in.
Castor angle	$1\frac{1}{2}°$	$1\frac{1}{2}°$
Camber angle	$1\frac{1}{2}°$	nil
King-pin inclination	$4°$ $47'$	$8°$
Lubrication		
Engine : Original S.A.E. grade	30	30
Quantity	8 pt.	9½ pt.
Gearbox : Original S.A.E. grade	30 (Flywheel: 30)	30 (Flywheel 30)
Quantity	4 pt. (Flywheel: 8 pt.)	5½ pt. (Flywheel 8 pt.)
Rear axle : Original S.A.E. grade	140 EP	90 HYP
Quantity	3 pt.	2½ pt.
Steering box : Original S.A.E. grade	140 EP	90 HYP
Tyres		
Size	6·50 x 15	6·70 x 15
Pressures (lb/in^2)	F : 26 R : 28	F : 26 R : 26

Lea-Francis '14'

1946-52. 1¾-litre Saloon. 4 seater

1950 Lea-Francis '14'

Lea-Francis engines were ohv designs with twin camshafts mounted high up at either side of the block; the inlet valves were actuated by one camshaft and the exhaust valves by the other. In this way, porting was completely unrestricted, and the spark plugs could be positioned between the inlet-and exhaust-ports. The short pushrods minimized the weight of the valve gear, wear being small and tappets keeping in correct adjustment for long periods of time. Also the entire valve gear could be removed with the cylinder head, thus simplifying dismantling. The '14' Saloon was powered by a four-cylinder engine of 1,767cc and 7.25 to 1 compression ratio, delivering 70 bhp at 4,700 rev/min and giving a top speed of 80 mile/h. In body design it was completely traditional but for the integral headlamps in the front wings; the upright, rectangular radiator grille dominated the straight lines of the narrow bonnet, and the roof area was large. Both front and rear wings were streamlined yet open, and the rear-window-and-boot line sloped downwards in a double curve. The bodywork was of pressed steel, and the chassis was unusual in that it was underslung at the rear. Front suspension was independent and by torsion bars, the rear being by leaf-springs. The interior was well appointed, with walnut fascia and window cappings, plus leather upholstery. Brakes were fully hydraulic, and a four-speed gearbox with central gear lever was fitted.

Features: Distinctive engine design of well-proven potential. Traditionally solid chassis and bodywork. Fully hydraulic brakes. Overall standard of finish very high.
Failings: All spares now hard to come by. Steel fabric must be preserved against rust.

Lea-Francis '2 ½-Litre'

1949-54 Sports. 2-4 seater

In 1949 Lea-Francis brought out two 2½-litre models, the 18 hp Saloon and the 2½-litre Sports. Both used the same engine, a four-cylinder in-line ohv design of 2,496cc and 7 to 1 compression ratio. The engine of the Sports, equipped with twin SU carburetters, produced 100 bhp at 4,000 rev/min. For competition use, special pistons could be fitted to raise the compression ratio to 7.63 to 1; this, together with a high-lift camshaft could raise the power to 120 bhp at 5,200 rev/min, and the top speed to 110 mile/h. In body shape (virtually a scaled-up version of the earlier postwar '14' Sports) the '2½-Litre' was an unusual design, with a diminutive and curved version of the traditional radiator grille, narrow tapering bonnet, and large enveloping front wings cut off at the rear. The rear wings were virtually of semi-circular shape, the rear wheels being closely faired-in. As in the '18' Saloon, the headlamps were integral with the front wings. A sturdy divided front bumper, large polished stone-deflectors on the faces of the rear wings, disc wheels, and a 'BMW 328'-type spare-wheel recess above the boot, were also distinctive features. The hood and tonneau cover folded away inside a special compartment behind the rear

1950 and 1951 Lea-Francis '2½-Litres'

seats, when not in use. Bodywork was of alloy and a high-tensile steel chassis was incorporated. Hydromechanical brakes were fitted on early models, this system soon being superceded by fully hydraulic brakes. Suspension pattern was independent on the front wheels by torsion bars, with leaf-springs on the rear. A four-speed Armstrong-Siddeley gearbox with central gear lever was fitted, power being transmitted to the rear wheels via an ENV axle.

Features: Distinctive engine and body design. Excellent performance from the modified engine. Alloy bodywork, sturdy chassis.
Failings: All body spares now hard to come by.

Car Club Honorary Secretary: David Purdy, 54 Gresham Way, Shefford, Beds.

SPARES: ('2½-litre' mechanics:) All available, through the Lea-Francis Owners' Club.
('2½-litre' body spares:) Non-existent; only source is through breakage.
('14' Saloon spares:) No details; probably very hard to come by — particularly body spares.

	Lea-Francis '14' Saloon	Lea-Francis '2½-Litre' Sports
Engine (Mechanical)		
No. of cylinders : capacity	4; 1,767 cc	4; 2,496 cc
Bore and stroke	75 x 100 mm	85 x 110 mm
Compression ratio	7·25 : 1	7 : 1
Valve layout	Overhead	Overhead
Tappet clearances	Inlet 0.004 in. Exhaust 0.006 in. (hot)	Inlet 0·010 in. Exhaust 0·012 in.
Location of valve timing marks	On flywheel	Boss on rocker box and locating-bar
Timing : inlet valve opens	10° btdc	15° btdc
Piston withdrawal direction	Downwards	Downwards
Engine (Ignition)		
Firing order	1, 3, 4, 2	1, 3, 4, 2
Location of timing marks	—	—
Timing : points open	5° btdc	2½° atdc
Original spark plugs	Lodge H14	Lodge H14
Plug gap	0.022—0.024 in.	0·020 in.
Original (Lucas) coil	Q12	B12
Original (Lucas) distributor	DKY4A	DVXH4A (vac. control)
Carburetters		
Original make	SU	2 SU
Original type	H4	H3
Jet size	0.09 in.	—
Metering Needle	Rich — AQ Standard EN	Rich No. 5
		Weak No. 3
Electrical Accessories		
Battery	12v 63 ah	12v 63 ah
Original (Lucas) generator	C45PV	C45PV/4
Original (Lucas) control box	RF95	RF95/2
Original (Lucas) starter motor	M418G	M45G

Lea-Francis '2½-Litre' at Lydden Circuit, 1971

	Lea-Francis '14' Saloon	Lea-Francis '2½-Litre' Sports
Chassis Components and Steering Geometry		
Brakes	Girling mechanical (later hydromechanical)	Girling hydromechanical (later hydraulic)
Rear axle : Type	Spiral bevel (later hypoid bevel)	Hypoid bevel
Ratio	4·88 : 1	3·64 : 1
Crown-wheel tooth contact	Adjustable by shims	Adjustable by screw thread
Front suspension	Semi-elliptic (later torsion bars)	Wishbones and torsion bars
Rear suspension	Semi-elliptic leaf	Semi-elliptic leaf
Steering Pattern	Worm and nut (later recirculating ball)	Worm and nut (later recirculating ball)
Toe-in	$1/16$ in.	$1/16 - 1/8$ in.
Castor angle	$2\frac{1}{2}°$	$2\frac{1}{2}°$
Camber angle	$1\frac{1}{2} - 2°$	$1\frac{1}{2}-2°$
King-pin inclination	$9°$	$9°$
Lubrication		
Engine : Original S.A.E. grade	Summer 30, Winter 20	Summer 30, Winter 20
Quantity	8½ pt.	12½ pt.
Gearbox : Original S.A.E. grade	50	50
Quantity	3½ pt.	3½ pt.
Rear axle : Original S.A.E. grade	140 EP or 90 HYP	90 HYP
Quantity	3 pt.	3 pt.
Steering box : Original S.A.E. grade	140 EP	90 EP
Tyres		
Size	5·25 or 5·50 x 17	6·00 x 16
Pressures (lb/in^2)	F : 24　　R : 24	F : 22　　R : 22

MG 'TC'

1946-49. 1¼-litre Sports. 2 seater

1949 MG 'TC'

After the war, the prewar 'TA' Series was continued as the 'TC', the basic design being deliberately little changed. The 1937 'TA' engine was of 1,292cc, of four-cylinder in-line pushrod overhead-valve pattern, developing 50 bhp at 4,500 rev/min. Compared with this, the 'TC's engine was of 1,250cc and developed 52 bhp at 5,000 rev/min. The pushrod overhead-valve design was retained. The bonnet line of the postwar 'Midgets' was lower, and the radiator less 'square and straight' in style than the 'TA'. The 'TC' was equipped with fully hydraulic brakes, a floor-change gearbox, and Bishop cam steering. The prewar TA became a symbol of the best in small capacity sports cars, often being seen in quantities in RAF Officers' car parks and on airfields. In the same way the 'TC' (and later the 'TD' and 'TF' Midgets) became a continuation of the wartime 'legend'. The square, upright radiator, long bonnet, open front mudguards, tiny cockpit with two distinct dashboards and 'chopped off' boot, still epitomize a whole era. The Midgets successfully retained a 'prewar British' air up until their disappearance in 1955.

Features: Basically orthodox, clean, 'British' mechanics. Small enough in dimensions for the amateur to restore in complete detail. Spares still readily available through several specialist dealers, and perhaps some through British Leyland. Good, solid chassis. A fanatically keen Car Club.

Failings: Anonymous examples appearing for sale may have been 'thrashed'. Ash frame for alloy bodywork may rot. Leaf-springs front and rear unprogressive.

MG 'YA' and 'YB'

1947-53. 1¼-litre Sports Saloon. 4 seater

Like the 'TC', the 'YA' and 'YB' were deliberate throw-backs; in this case to the prewar 'Magnette 'KN' and '1½-Litre'. The engine used in both was the same as that fitted in the 'TC' and 'TD', *i.e.* a four-cylinder in-line pushrod ohv unit of 1,250cc developing 50 bhp, carburation being supplied by a single SU carburetter. In outward appearance the 'YA' and 'YB' retained the 'upright squareness' of their prewar ancestors. The long bonnet etc. of the 'TC' was echoed exactly in the 'Y's; differences in body shape began at the scuttle, and rearwards of this line the style of the body had little in common with the two-seaters. The 'YA' had a spiral bevel rear axle while the later 'YB' was fitted with a hypoid type. Suspension was by independent coil on the front wheels and leaf-springs on the rear. Fully hydraulic brakes and a rack-and-pinion steering box were incorporated, both forward-looking features. In all, the 'YA' and 'YB' were interesting cars — a compromise between the comfort of a saloon and the verve of a sports car. Top speed was 75 mile/h, whereas the 'TC' could exceed 80 mile/h.

1951 MG 'YB'

Features: As for the 'TC', More comfortable and more waterproof, but a much larger area of bodywork to maintain.

Failings: Extra weight of the saloon body takes the edge off the performance. Single carburetter limits acceleration. Definitely not as much fun as the open MGs.

Car Club Honorary Secretary: G. Gordon Cobban, P.O. Box 16, Westminster Bank Chambers, Abingdon, Berks.

('T' Register:) B. Lacey-Malvern, 7 Truro Drive, Exeter EX4 20Y

SPARES: 1. S.H. Richardson & Sons Ltd, Moor Lane, Staines, Middx.

2. NTG, Gateway Cottage, Holton-St.-Mary, Colchester.

3. Toulmins Ltd, 181, London Rd, Isleworth.

4. (Spares and fibreglass wings:) Octagon Sports Cars Ltd., 19-21, Grosvenor Park Rd., E. 17. (01-521 0520)

5. Archway Engineering Ltd., Collier St, Liverpool Rd, Manchester 3. (061-834 6455)

6. (Gearbox:) Briton Engineering, Croydon. (01-631 0633)

7. (Chrome parts:) Kimble Engineering Ltd, 8 Painswick Rd, Birmingham 28 (021-777 2011).

8. (Hoods:) London Trimming Co. Ltd, Store 'F', Marshgate Estate, Taplow, Nr. Maidenhead, Berks.

9. (Hoods by post) A.C. Winmill, 49 Tonstall Rd, Mitcham, Surrey.

	M.G. 'TC' Sports	M.G. 'YA', 'YB' Saloons
Engine (Mechanical)		
No. of cylinders : capacity	4; 1,250 cc	4; 1,250 cc
Bore and stroke	66·5 x 90 mm	66·5 x 90 mm
Compression ratio	7·25 : 1	7·2 : 1
Valve layout	Pushrod ohv	Pushrod ohv
Tappet clearances	0·019 in. (hot)	0·019 in. (hot)
Location of valve timing marks	On sprocket and chain bright links	On sprocket and chain bright links
Timing : inlet valve opens	11° btdc	11° btdc
Piston withdrawal direction	Downwards	Downwards
Engine (Ignition)		
Firing order	1, 3, 4, 2	1, 3, 4, 2
Location of timing marks	On timing cover and pulley rim	On timing cover and pulley rim
Timing : points open	tdc fully retarded	tdc fully retarded
Original spark plugs	Champion L10S	Champion L10S
Plug gap	0·022 in.	0·022 in.
Original (Lucas) coil	Q12	Q12
Original (Lucas) distributor	DKY4A	DKY4A
Carburetters		
Original make	2 SU	SU
Original type	H2	H2
Jet size	0·090 in.	0·090 in.
Metering needle	ES	FI
Electrical Accessories		
Battery	12v 51 ah	12v 50 ah
Original (Lucas) generator	C39PV	C45YV/3
Original (Lucas) control box	RF95	RB106/1
Original (Lucas) starter motor	M418G	M35G

	M.G. 'TC' Sports	M.G. 'YA', 'YB' Saloons
Chassis Components and Steering Geometry		
Brakes	Lockheed hydraulic	Lockheed hydraulic
Rear axle : Type	Spiral bevel	YA : Spiral bevel
		YB : Hypoid bevel
Ratio	5·125 : 1	YA : 5·143 : 1
		YB : 5·125 : 1
Crown-wheel tooth contact	Adjustable by shims and bearing nuts	YA : Adjustable by bearing nuts
		YB : Adjustable by spacers
Front suspension	Semi-elliptic leaf	Independent coil
Rear suspension	Semi-elliptic leaf	Semi-elliptic leaf
Steering Pattern	Bishop cam	Rack and pinion
Toe-in	$3/32$ in.	Nil
Castor angle	$5\frac{1}{2}°$	$1°$
Camber angle	$10\frac{1}{2}°$	Nil
King-pin inclination	$7\frac{1}{2}°$	$10°$
Lubrication		
Engine : Original S.A.E. grade	30	30
Quantity	9 pt.	9 pt.
Gearbox : Original S.A.E. grade	140 EP	YA : 140, YB : 90 HYP
Quantity	1½ pt.	1¼ pt.
Rear axle : Original S.A.E. grade	140 EP	YA : 140, YB : 90 HYP
Quantity	2 pt.	YA : 1½ pt. YB : 2pt.
Steering box : Original S.A.E. grade	140 EP	YA : 140, YB : 90 HYP
Tyres		
Size	5·50 x 15	5·50 x 15
Pressures (lb/in^2)	F : 24 R : 26	F : 23 R : 25

1949 MG 'TC'

Morgan '4/4' Series I

1945-50. 1¼-litre Sports. 2 seater

The basic body design of all four-wheeler Morgans remained virtually unchanged from 1936 to 1952. The earliest, the '4/4', was a basically simple, clean design with large open mudguards, longish tapering bonnet with plenty of louvres and a flat, slightly angled radiator. In 1945 there remained still a choice of two types of engine: a Coventry-Climax 1,122cc unit or a Standard 'Ten' unit of 1,267cc, the latter being by far the most common. The Standard 'Ten' unit employed a compression ratio of 7 to 1, and was of ohv pattern giving a top speed in the 70s. By 1947, however, Standards announced their intention of producing one engine only, that for the future 'Vanguard', and this powerplant was to make possible the new 'Plus 4' Morgan of 1950. The '4/4' and 'Plus 4' remained unique in that they retained the traditional Morgan feature of a gearbox separate from the engine and linked by an enclosed tunnel. The gearbox had four speeds with floor-mounted lever. Fully mechanical brakes and worm-and-nut steering were employed; suspension pattern was of independent coil on the front wheels and leaf-springs on the rear. Body fabric

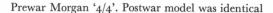

Prewar Morgan '4/4'. Postwar model was identical

was of steel with an ash frame, and a true chassis was incorporated. The cock pit itself was a little cramped and the boot merely a small box accessible by tilting the seats. Roadholding qualities were good and steering light, yet very positive. The '4/4' Series II of 1956 had a Ford 100E engine.

Features: Compact enough for complete renovation by an amateur. Consistent Morgan body design — helpful when seeking body spares. Realistic fuel consumption. Very keen Car Club.

Failings: Coventry-Climax engine obscure and costly to rebuild; Standard engine possibly a little easier. Fully mechanical brakes poor for the 1970s. Wooden structural details may rot. Steel bodywork must be maintained. Primitive front suspension exposed to road mud (Series I only).

Morgan 'Plus 4'

1950-55. 2-litre Sports. 2-seater

In 1950 the higher-powered 'Plus 4' appeared. At first a Standard 'Vanguard' engine of 2,088cc was fitted. Its compression ratio was 6.7 to 1 and it developed 68 bhp at 4,200 rev/min, giving a top speed of 85 mile/h and a fuel consumption of 25 mpg. These first 'Plus 4' models resembled the '4/4' but were wider, had a longer bonnet and a lower, but still flat radiator. In 1953 the entire frontal design was changed: the separate chromed headlamps were dispensed with and blended into the front wings which now covered the front suspension, while the radiator was repositioned behind a curved, sloping grille. Then, in 1954, a modified Triumph 'TR2' engine was fitted as an alternative to the 'Vanguard' engine. It was of 1,991cc and 8.5 to 1 compression ratio, developing 90 bhp at 4,800 rev/min. Top speed by the mid-fifties was around 100 mile/h. Brakes were fully hydraulic and suspension pattern identical to the '4/4'. A Moss four-speed gearbox was fitted (as in pre-and XK Jaguars). Chassis design was of boxed Z-section ladder type. Steering was changed in 1954 to cam-and-sect or pattern, but suspension remained traditionally Morgan, *i.e.* firm. By 1955 the twin spare wheels, aimed at attracting trials enthusiasts, ceased to be fitted.

Features: A much faster car than the '4/4' ('TR' engine.) Hydraulic brakes (discs on front from 1954). Engine spares not too difficult still. Or used spares may be obtained from scrapped 'TR 2's, 'TR 3's, or Phase I 'Vanguards'.

Failings: Steel bodywork with ash frame needs maintenance. Certainly a 'hard' ride. No room for air-cleaners under the cramped bonnet.

Car Club Honorary Secretary: C.J. Smith, 23 Seymour Ave, Worcester.
(Morgan Register:) T.H. L. Cree, 3 Ashendon Close, Droitwich, Worcs.

SPARES: 1. Stapleton Bros, South Kensington. (01-589 6894.)

2. Allon White & Son Ltd, Cranfield, Beds. (Cranfield 205 or 314).

3. ('Standard' engines:) A.T. Johnson, Paradise Rd, Downham Market, Norfolk (Downham Market 3407/8).

4. Standard-Triumph stockists, to a degree.

5. Through above club.

	Morgan '4/4' Series I	Morgan 'Plus 4' ('Vanguard' engine*)
Engine (Mechanical)		
No. of cylinders : capacity	4; 1,267 cc	4; 2,088 cc
Bore and stroke	63·5 x 100 mm	85 x 92 mm
Compression ratio	7 : 1	6·7 : 1 (1954-5, 7 : 1)
Valve layout	Overhead	Overhead
Tappet clearances	0·022 in. (cold)	Inlet 0·010 in. Exhaust 0·012 in. (cold)
Location of valve timing marks	On chainwheel	On sprocket and camshaft
Timing : inlet valve opens	10° btdc	10° btdc
Piston withdrawal direction	Downwards	Upwards
Engine (Ignition)		
Firing order	1, 3, 4, 2	1, 3, 4, 2
Location of timing marks	On flywheel	tdc indicator
Timing : points open	tdc	4° btdc
Original spark plugs	Champion NA8	Champion L10
Plug gap	0·025 in.	0·032 in.
Original (Lucas) distributor	DKY4A	DM2/V164
Carburetters		
Original make	Solex	Solex
Original type	30 FAI	32 BI
Choke tube	26 or 30	25
Main jet	125	140
Compensating jet	170	—
Slow-running jet	45	55
Electrical Accessories		
Battery	12v 57 ah	12v 57 ah
Original (Lucas) generator	C45NV/L	C39PV/2
Original (Lucas) control box	CFR2/L14	RF96/2
Original (Lucas) starter motor	M35A	M418G
Chassis Components and Steering Geometry		
Brakes	Girling mechanical	Girling hydraulic
Rear axle : Type	Spiral bevel	Hypoid bevel
Ratio	4·72 : 1	1950-53, 4·1 : 1 1954-56, 3·7 : 1
Front suspension	Independent coil and sliding pillar	Independent coil and sliding pillar
Rear suspension	Semi-elliptic leaf	Semi-elliptic leaf
Steering Pattern	Worm and nut	1950-53 Worm and nut 1954-56 Cam and sector
Toe-in	$^{1}/_{8}$ in.	$^{1}/_{8} - {}^{3}/_{16}$ in.
Castor angle	4°	4°
Camber angle	2°	2°
King-pin inclination	2°	2°

*For alternative engine data refer to Triumph 'TR2' engine in Triumph section

1954 Morgan 'Plus 4'

	Morgan '4/4' Series I	Morgan 'Plus 4' ('Vanguard' engine*)
Lubrication		
Engine : Original S.A.E. grade	Summer 30, Winter 20	Summer 30, Winter 20
Quantity	8 pt.	11 pt.
Gearbox : Original S.A.E. grade	90 EP	30
Quantity	1½ pt.	2½ pt.
Rear axle : Original S.A.E. grade	140 EP	90 HYP
Quantity	1½ pt.	2½ pt.
Steering box : Original S.A.E. grade	140 EP	90 HYP
Tyres		
Size	4·50 x 17	5·25 x 16
Pressures (lb/in²)	F : 18 R : 20	F : 16 R : 18

Riley 'RMA' and 'RME'

1945-55. 1½-litre Saloon. 4 seater

Riley were taken over by Morris in 1938, hence a certain amount of individuality was sacrificed from then onwards. The first RMA model (probably designed pre-1938) appeared in 1946, combining the classic pre-war lines with a certain degree of streamlining. The characteristic Riley bonnet was retained, but the headlamps were blended into the front wings; in general the postwar design looked far less angular and awkward. The engine was of four-cylinder in-line inclined ohv pattern, and of 1,496cc capacity, the compression ratio being 6.8 to 1. By 1955 the RME engine developed 56 bhp at 4,500 rev/min, giving a top speed of 77 mile/h. Riley 'Torsionic' torsion-bar suspension for the front wheels and leaf-springs for the rear was employed; steering was of rack-and-pinion design. A floor-change gearbox was fitted, with four forward gears. Bodywork was of pressed steel, excepting a fabric-type roof section and aluminium bonnet lids; the chassis was of welded I-section steel channel. RMA type numbers had the following prefixes: 1946 — 36S, 1947 — 37S, 1948 — 38S, etc. up to 1952 — 42S; after 1952 the prefix was omitted and RME substituted. At the 1953 Motor Show the new RME offered re-styled wings and sills, with wheel-covers at the rear. The RME had an RMA engine with modified high-lift

1947 Riley 'RMA'

cams. 1946-52 models had 'torque tube' drive; the RME had a hypoid axle from chassis No. 42520505. Models of 1946-50 had hydromechanical brakes; fully hydraulic brakes were introduced in Oct. 1952 at chassis No. 42520505, also. An AC mechanical fuel pump was fitted on early 1946 models, after which an SU electric pump was substituted (from chassis 37S-2169).

Features: Sturdy chassis. Spares readily available through specialists, and many through original equipment manufacturers. Fairly orthodox 'British' straight-four design. Torque tube models very stable on corners. 'Torsionic' suspension gives a very comfortable ride. Fairly economical on fuel. Original finish of paintwork superb.

Failings: Steel bodywork susceptible to rusting at bottom of rear door pillars and floor of boot. Fabric top and wooden frame will rot if not maintained. Open propshaft models tend to break away on corners. Engine gets very dirty. Engine compartment cramped.

Riley 'RMB'

1946-53. 2½-litre Saloon. 4-5 seater

The development of the 'RMB 1' and 'RMB 2' ran parallel with that of the 'RMA'; the 'RMF' appeared with the 'RME', after 1952. The 'RMB' engine was of four-cylinder in-line inclined ohv pattern and of 2,443cc capacity. The 'RMB 1' engine produced 100 bhp at 4,500 rev/min, its compression ratio being 6.8 to 1. The maximum speed of the production model was 95 mile/h, but present-day enthusiasts have, by re-working and very fine tuning, raised this top speed into the region of 110-128 mile/h. The entire car was very solidly built, and in many ways was a 'scaled up' version of the 'RMA'. For identification purposes the 'RMB' type-numbers had the following prefixes: 1946—56S, 1947—57S, etc. up to 1952—62S. After 1952 the prefix was omitted and 'RMF' substituted, and at the 1953 Motor Show the 'RMF' was replaced by the 'Pathfinder'. The bodywork of the 'RMB' was of pressed steel except for the bonnet covers, which were of aluminium. A sturdy chassis was used, together with Riley 'Torsionic' torsion bar suspension on the front wheels; leaf-springs were fitted for the rear wheels. Hydromechanical brakes and a rack-and-pinion steering box were incorporated. The 'RMB' retained the 'floor change' type of gear lever.

Features: As for the 'RMA'. A much faster car, however. Good, solid construction throughout. Comfortable ride plus high performance.

Failings: Steel bodywork susceptible to rusting if not maintained. Rather a heavy car for the type of brakes fitted. Gearbox ratios very high — poor pulling away on hills. Half-shafts tend to fail (cured on 'RMF'). Engine gets dirty, engine compartment cramped.

Car Club Honorary Secretary: A. Farrar, The Gables, Hinksey Hill, Oxford, OX1 5BH.

('R.M. Club':) D.J. Morris, 126 Coventry Road, Market Harborough, Leicestershire.

SPARES: 1. Riley dealers, to a degree.

2. Lundergaard Ltd., 71-73, Southgate, Gloucester.

3. B.H. Renwick, 'Bracken', Water Lane, Golant, Fowey, Cornwall, (Fowey 2229).

4. Through above club.

	Riley 'RMA', 'RME'	Riley 'RMB'
Engine (Mechanical)		
No. of cylinders : capacity	4; 1,496 cc	4; 2,443 cc
Bore and stroke	69 x 100 mm	80·5 x 120 mm
Compression ratio	6·8 : 1	6·8 : 1
Valve layout	Inclined overhead	Inclined overhead
Tappet clearances	Inlet 0·003 in.	Inlet 0·003 in.
	Exhaust 0·004 in. (hot)	Exhaust 0·004 in. (hot)
Location of valve timing marks	Crankshaft keyway and marks on camshaft wheel	Crankshaft keyway and marks on camshaft wheel
Timing : inlet valve opens	9° btdc	17° btdc
Piston withdrawal direction	Upwards	Upwards
Engine (Ignition)		
Firing order	1, 2, 4, 3	1, 2, 4, 3
Location of timing marks	—	—
Timing : points open	8° btdc, fully advanced	4-8° btdc, fully advanced
Original spark plugs	Champion L10S	Champion NA8
Plug gap	0·025 in.	0·025 in.
Original (Lucas) coil	B12	B12
Original (Lucas) distributor	DKY4A	DKY4A
Carburetters		
Original make	SU	2 SU
Original type	H2	H4
Metering needle	No. 3	EE
Electrical Accessories		
Battery	12v 51 ah	12v 63 ah
Original (Lucas) generator	C39PV	C45PV/14
Original (Lucas) control box	RF91 (later RF95)	RF95
Original (Lucas) starter motor	M418G	M45G
Chassis Components and Steering Geometry		
Brakes	Girling hydromechanical/hydraulic	Girling hydromechanical
Rear axle : Type	Spiral bevel (later hypoid)	Spiral bevel (later hypoid)
Ratio	4·89 : 1	4·1 : 1
Crown-wheel tooth contact	Adjustable by shims	Adjustable by shims
Front suspension	Torsion bars	Torsion bars
Rear suspension	Semi-elliptic leaf	Semi-elliptic leaf
Steering Pattern	Rack and pinion	Rack and pinion
Toe-in	Nil	Nil
Castor angle	3°	3°
Camber angle	1°	1°
King-pin inclination	11°	11°

1951 Riley 'RMB'

	Riley 'RMA', 'RME'	Riley 'RMB'
Lubrication		
Engine : Original S.A.E. grade	30	30
Quantity	10 pt.	14 pt.
Gearbox : Original S.A.E. grade	140 EP	140 EP
Quantity	2 pt.	2 pt.
Rear axle : Original S.A.E. grade	140 EP or 90 HYP	140 EP or 90 HYP
Quantity	2¾ pt.	4 pt.
Steering box : Original S.A.E. grade	Medium grease	Medium grease
Tyres		
Size	5·75 x 16	6·00 x 16
Pressures (lb/in^2)	F : 22 R : 24	F : 24 R : 24

Rover P3-'60'

1948-49. 1½-litre Saloon. 4-5 seater

1948 Rover P3-'60'

In 1948 the short-lived P3—'60' and '75' Series appeared, direct forerunners to the famous P4 Series. Basically they consisted of the 1945-47 body (of distinctively prewar style) in which a new design of engine was substituted. This new engine design was to become a basic part of the P4, having an ioe F-head (overhead inlet coupled with side exhaust valves). But as regards outward appearances, the P3s were still basically a continuation of the Rover saloons of the late 1930s, retaining a certain 'angular' flavour. The headlamps and the sidelamps remained independent of the open front wings; the boot was box-like with squarish corners; the bonnet long and tapering. The 4-cylinder P3-'60' engine was of 1,595cc and 7.05 to 1 compression ratio, developing 50 bhp at 4,000 rev/min and giving a top speed of 78 mile/h approximately. Fuel consumption was in the order of 24-33 mpg. It was obvious that a new type of engine needed to be complemented by a new design in bodywork, —hence in 1949 the P4 appeared.

Features: Robust design. Sturdy chassis. Engine spares still available through certain specialists. Distinctive engine design; reasonable fuel consumption.

Failings: Body spares difficult (short-lived style). Bodywork needs careful maintenance.

Rover P4-'75'

1949-54. 2-litre Saloon. 4-5 seater

The P4 Series represented an entirely new body design and incorporated an improved chassis structure. The first P4—'75' used the P3-type six-cylinder engine with its 'F'-head now cast in alloy, a capacity of 2,103cc, and power output of 75 bhp at 4,200 rev/min. Its compression ratio was 7.25 to 1, and it was fed by twin SU carburetters; in 1954 the engine capacity was increased to 2,230cc. This later unit developed 80 bhp at 4,500 rev/min; its carburation differed in that a single SU carburetter only was employed. The maximum speed was 87 mile/h, and fuel consumption 20-30 mpg. The gearbox operation of the '75' was of two types: 1949-52 models were fitted with a gear lever mounted on the steering column, while models of 1952-54 employed a gearbox with a 'floor change' lever. Spiral bevel final drive, fully hydraulic brakes (from 1951) and independent coil front suspension were used, and all the '75's were fitted with the Rover 'freewheel' which enabled the driver to change gear without using the clutch and also to save fuel. In body design the P4 Series broke free from the prewar 'shackles' of earlier styles — here was a design for the Fifties, flowing of line, yet still rugged in its streamlining. The tall radiator grille of the P3 gave way to a wider, squarer shape with central fog-lamp, the grille being blended into the front wings along with the headlamps; the wings, however, were kept open enough to cover very little of the wheels and this contributed further to the design's overall 'smooth ruggedness'. Aluminium panels were used for the boot lid, doors and bonnet lid; the rest of the bodywork was in pressed steel. The interior featured two leather-covered bench seats, floor carpets, and dashboard and door-cappings finished in walnut. Changes in design were incorporated during the five years of its manufacture as follows: in 1950 the dashboard was re-designed with circular, instead of square dials; by 1952 the grille became elongated horizontally and the 'cyclops' fog-lamp was omitted; in 1953 synchronized second gear became standard; in 1954 a wider 3-piece rear window appeared.

Features: Sturdy body and chassis. Distinctive engine design, superbly built, giving very long service. Excellent degree of comfort. Interior finish of a very high standard.

Failings: Alloy cylinder heads require great care in fitting. Rubber oil seals in valve guides should be replaced regularly to prevent oil being burnt in cylinders. Rather a 'thirsty' engine when elderly. Steel body panels require constant maintenance.

Car Club Honorary Secretary: T.L.J. Bentley, 11 Woodhall Drive, Pinner, Middx.

SPARES: 1. Through Rover dealers, to a degree.
         2. Roverpart, 320 Brockley Road, Lewisham, London, SE4.
         3. Motolympia, Welshpool, Montgomeryshire (Welshpool 2327).

	Rover P3 — '60'	Rover P4 — '75'
Engine (Mechanical)		
No. of cylinders : capacity	4; 1,595 cc	6; 2,103 cc
Bore and stroke	69·5 x 105 mm	65·2 x 105 mm
Compression ratio	7·05 : 1	7·25 : 1
Valve layout	Overhead inlet, side exhaust	Overhead inlet, side exhaust
Tappet clearances	Inlet 0·010 in.	Inlet 0·008 in.
	Exhaust 0·012 in. (hot)	Exhaust 0·012 in. (hot)
Location of valve timing marks	On flywheel (EP) and on clutch housing	On flywheel (EP) and on clutch housing
Timing : inlet valve opens	9° btdc	9° btdc
Piston withdrawal direction	Upwards (first turn in bore 90°) Conrods downwards	Upwards (first turn in bore 90°) Conrods downwards
Engine (Ignition)		
Firing order	1,3,4,2	1,5,3,6,2,4
Location of timing marks	On flywheel (FA) and on clutch housing	On flywheel (FA) and on clutch housing
Timing : points open	11° btdc	8° btdc
Original spark plugs	Lodge HLNR	Lodge HLNR
Plug gap	0·023–0·026 in.	0·023–0·026 in.
Original (Lucas) coil	B12	HV12
Original (Lucas) distributor	DVXH4A	DMBZ6A
Carburetters		
Original make	Solex	2 SU
Original type	32PB12	H4
Choke tube	23	1½ in.
Main jet	102·5	Metering needle FV or GE
Compensating jet	160	Jet size 0·090 in.
Slow-running jet	45	—
Pump jet	55	—
Electrical Accessories		
Battery	12v 51 ah	12v 51 ah
Original (Lucas) generator	C45PV/5	45PV/5
Original (Lucas) control box	RF95/2	RB106/1
Original (Lucas) starter motor	M418G	M418G
Chassis Components and Steering Geometry		
Brakes	Girling hydromechanical	1949-51 : Girling hydromechanical 1951-54 : Girling hydraulic
Rear axle : Type	Spiral bevel	Spiral bevel
Ratio	4·7 : 1	4·3 : 1
Crown-wheel tooth contact	Adjustable by nuts and shims	Adjustable by nuts and shims
Front suspension	Independent coil	Independent coil
Rear suspension	Semi-elliptic leaf	Semi-elliptic leaf
Steering pattern	Worm and nut	Burman recirculating ball
Toe-in	0–⅛ in.	0–⅛ in.
Castor angle	4–6°	2° negative
Camber angle	½–2°	1–3°
King-pin inclination	6–8°	2½–4½°

1951 Rover P4-'75'

	Rover P3 – '60'		Rover P4 – '75'	
Lubrication				
Engine : Original S.A.E. grade	Summer 30, Winter 20		Summer 30, Winter 20	
Quantity	10 pt.		15 pt.	
Gearbox : Original S.A.E. grade	50		20	
Quantity	4 pt.		3½ pt.	
Rear axle : Original S.A.E. grade	90 EP		90 EP	
Quantity	3 pt.		2½ pt.	
Steering box : Original S.A.E. grade	140 EP		140 EP	
Tyres				
Size	5·25 x 17		6·00 x 15	
Pressures (lb/in^2)	F : 27	R : 27	F : 28	R : 24

Sunbeam-Talbot '90' Mk 1

1948-50. 2-litre Sports Saloon. 4 seater

1950 Sunbeam-Talbot '90' Mk I

The Rootes Group took over the London division of the Clement Talbot Company in 1935; the residual French Talbot concern was re-named Talbot-Lago after Tony Lago had gained direction of it. Rootes named their newly acquired 'takeover' Sunbeam-Talbot by amalgamating it with one of their existing companies. In 1945 the 1.2-litre sv 'Ten' appeared, a continuation of their prewar-style product. Shortly after this, work began on a new series of more modern design, to be powered by ohv engines; Ted White was chief of the design team and Raymond Lowry developed the body styling. By 1948 the first two models, the '80' and '90' Mk I reached production. They were at once a success, their design having flowing yet compact lines, typifying a new era in body trends, and this was combined with an attractive performance. The rectangular, uncompromising prewar radiator grille now emerged from aerodynamic front wings allied to a curving bonnet, the compact, economical lines of the body ending in a rather 'tubby' boot still reminiscent of Talbots of the late 1930s. The '90', the higher-powered of the two, was fitted with a four-cylinder in-line ohv engine of 1,944cc, developing 64 bhp at 4,100 rev/min, and giving a top speed of 75-80 mile/h. A sturdy chassis and pressed steel bodywork were employed, and both the '80' and '90' were equipped with fully hydraulic brakes, the suspension at first relying on leaf-springs front and rear. A four-speed gearbox with column-mounted gear lever was installed in both models. Steering pattern was worm-and-nut; the earlier type of spiral bevel rear axle was fitted. (The '90' Mk II was fitted with independent coil front suspension, and this and the Mk. IIa were from 1950 powered by 2,267cc engines, the increased power making the design one of the most sprightly saloons available at the time, and very suitable for competition work. Its successor, the Sunbeam 'Mk III' of 1954-57, won the Monte Carlo Rally in 1955.)

1951 Sunbeam-Talbot '90' Mk II Convertible

Features: Orthodox, straight-four 'British' engine. Compact, timeless body shape. True chassis fitted. Fully hydraulic brakes. Virtually all spares still readily available (see addresses below).

Failings: Solid bodywork and chassis, but both demand constant maintenance. Gearbox noisy after long mileage and 'jumps out' on the over-run. Gear-change mechanism wears rather rapidly. King-pins rather short and also wear. Car over-bodied.

Sunbeam 'Alpine'

1953-55. 2¼-litre Sports Convertible. 2 seater

The 'Alpine' was derived from the basic body shape of the '90' Mk IIa saloon, and introduced in March 1953 as the Mk 1 'Alpine'. Around this period the Sunbeam-Talbot name was shortened to merely 'Sunbeam', the Rootes Group wishing to differentiate between their products and the Talbot-Lago concern. (Since, however, the same shaped bonnet motif was still employed, this was deceptive to a degree; closer examination revealed that in fact the word 'Sunbeam' was reiterated on either side. The model was never called a 'Sunbeam-Talbot Alpine'). The engine fitted in the Mk I 'Alpine' was a tuned version of the Mk IIa unit; it was of four-cylinder in-line ohv pattern and 2,267cc capacity, developing 80 bhp at 4,200 rev/min, an increase of 10 bhp on the basic 'IIa' engine. The top speed of the Mk I 'Alpine' in standard trim was approximately 95 mile/h. It was of exceptionally clean lines, if

1953 Sunbeam 'Alpine' Mk I

anything improving upon those of its saloon ancestor. The form of the front wings, taken straight from the '90', swept back through the door panels to finally merge imperceptibly into the rear wheel arches. The rear wings emerged in a very subtle way from a high bonnet line that extended from front to rear. Two long rows of louvres ran along both sides of the bonnet top; the solid wheels were perforated with a row of circular holes which while enhancing the appearance also served as cooling for the brake drums. Outwardly, the 'Alpine' was the epitome of compactness allied with clean, balanced proportions. In 1954 there appeared the new Sunbeam 'Mk III' Series saloon, four-seater convertible, and 'Mk III Alpine'; all three used the same tuned-up Mk IIa engine of 7.5 to 1 compression ratio. An optional speed kit was available for all 'Mk III' models, the engine then developing 92 bhp and providing increased performance, while the even more powerful engine of the Sunbeam Alpine 'Special' (a factory-tuned version with straight-through exhaust and Solex twin-choke carburetter) delivered 97 bhp and gave a top speed of 104 mile/h. All 'Alpines' had steel bodywork, supported by a sturdy chassis; a four-speed gearbox with column-mounted gear lever was fitted; fully hydraulic brakes, and independent coil front suspension together with leaf-springs for the rear, were used. As in the '90' Mk. II and Mk. IIa, the rear axle was of the hypoid type. Steering gear was of recirculating-ball pattern. With its attractive, timeless body design and excellent performance, the 'Alpine' remains a very worthwhile investment.

Features: As for the '90', plus added performance. Rugged chassis and bodywork. Engine bulky but accessible, and extremely reliable. Optional overdrive may be fitted for economical high-speed cruising. Well-appointed interior. Often 'tatty-looking' examples are perfectly serviceable mechanically.

Failings: Steel bodywork and chassis do have corroding tendencies (the latter in the area of the rear spring anchorages) and demand maintenance. Gearbox, as with the '90', tends to become noisy after prolonged mileage and 'jumps out' on the over-run. Gear-change mechanism wears unduly, as do the king-pins. Clutch judder common; differentials can sometimes fail.

Car Club Honorary Secretary: No official club recognized by the RAC.(Sunbeam-Talbot and Alpine Register:) D. Elsbury, 12 Everest Rd, Fishponds, Bristol.

SPARES: 1. C. Moar, Rosehall Works, North Rd, Shawhead, Coatbridge, Lanarkshire, Scotland.
2. John M. Bland, 27 Southfields Rd, London SW18 (01-874 1612)
3. (Gearboxes:) Caterham 44308; Barking 594-3374.
4. R.J. Grimes, Hadleigh Garage, Marlpit Lane, Coulsdon, Surrey.
5. Through above club.

1953 Sunbeam 'Alpine' Mk I

	Sunbeam-Talbot '90' Mk I	Sunbeam 'Alpine'
Engine (Mechanical)		
No. of cylinders : capacity	4; 1,944 cc	4; 2,267 cc
Bore and stroke	75 x 110 mm	81 x 110 mm
Compression ratio	6·69 : 1	6·5 or 7·5 : 1
Valve layout	Overhead	Overhead
Tappet clearances	Inlet 0·007 in. Exhaust 0·009 in.	Inlet 0·007 in. Exhaust 0·009 in.
Location of valve timing marks	Dots on timing wheels	Dots on timing wheels
Timing : inlet valve opsn	13° btdc	19° btdc
Piston withdrawal direction	Downwards	Upwards
Engine (Ignition)		
Firing order	1, 3, 4, 2	1, 3, 4, 2
Location of timing marks	tdc 1 and 4 mark on flywheel	tdc 1 and 4 mark on flywheel
Timing : points open	1° btdc	1° btdc
Original spark plugs	Champion NA8	Champion NA8
Plug gap	0·028–0·032 in.	0·028–0·032 in.
Original (Lucas) coil	B12/LO	B12/LO
Original (Lucas) distributor	DVXH4A	DVXHBQ31
Carburetters		
Original make	Stromberg	Stromberg
Original type	DBA 36	DBA 36 or DI 36
Choke tube	1^1/16 in.	1^3/32 in. 1^3/16 in.
Main jet	0·052	0·052 0·060
Compensating jet	0·030	0·030 0·044
Slow-running jet	75-68	75-70 (and pump jet 75)
Electrical Accessories		
Battery	12v 51 ah	12v 51 ah
Original (Lucas) generator	C45PV/3-4	C45PV/3-4 or C45 PV/5
Original (Lucas) control box	RF95/L2	RF95/2L4 or RB106/1
Original (Lucas) starter motor	M418G/LO	M418G
Chassis Components and Steering Geometry		
Brakes	Lockheed hydraulic	Lockheed hydraulic
Rear axle : Type	Spiral bevel	Hypoid bevel
Ratio	4·3 : 1	3·9 : 1 or 4·22 : 1
Crown-wheel tooth contact	Adjustable	Adjustable by shims
Front suspension	Semi-elliptic leaf	Independent coil
Rear suspension	Semi-elliptic leaf	Semi-elliptic leaf
Steering pattern	Worm and nut	Recirculating ball
Toe-in	1/8 in.	1/8 in.
Castor angle	4° laden	3° laden
Camber angle	1½° laden	¾° laden
King-pin inclination	7½° laden	8¼° laden
Lubrication		
Engine : Original S.A.E. grade	30	30
Quantity	10½ pt.	10½ pt.
Gearbox : Original S.A.E. grade	30	30
Quantity	2 pt.	2 pt. or 2¼ pt.
Rear axle : Original S.A.E. grade	140 EP	90 HYP
Quantity	1 pt.	1¾ pt.
Steering box : Original S.A.E. grade	140 EP	140 EP
Tyres		
Size	5·25 x 16	5·50 x 16
Pressures (lb/in^2)	F : 24 R : 26	F : 22 R : 28

Triumph '1800' and '2000'

1946-49. 1¾-litre and 2-litre Roadster. 3-5 seater

1948 Triumph '1800' Roadster. Note dickey-seats

The Standard Motor Company supplied engines to SS Cars Ltd., (which after the war became Jaguar Cars) from 1931, to power their tourers and two-seaters, the latter being the SS '90' and legendary SS '100' Jaguars. In 1945, Standard acquired the Triumph Company and formed a subsidiary, the Triumph Motor Company Ltd. This new company's first cars were the 1946 '1800' Roadster and Saloon. To power them both, a 1¾-litre engine was employed which had originally been built for SS Cars Ltd. Excess production offered a perfect opportunity to use this powerplant in a new sports design. Of four-cylinder in line ohv type, 1,776cc capacity and 6.72 to 1 compression ratio, this unit developed 63 bhp at 4,500 rev/min, giving the 'Roadster' a top speed of 80 mile/h. A very long, tapering bonnet and traditional chromed radiator shell, large bulbous front wings protruding in front of the radiator, separate chromed headlamps and twin horns, and a high 'tail' concealing two dickey-seats, were characteristic features. A flat, glass-paned metal panel in front of the boot lid could be raised to serve as a windscreen for the passengers in the dickey-seats. A rugged tubular chassis supported the ash-framed aluminium bodywork (the front wings only were in pressed steel.) A four-speed gearbox was operated by a 'right-hand' column-mounted gear lever; the suspension relied entirely on leaf-springs front and rear. The braking system was hydrastatic and the rear axle of the earlier spiral bevel type. Steering pattern was cam-and-double-roller. The 16in. balloon tyres and simple, but very effective suspension gave a comfortable and very smooth ride. From 1949 a Standard 'Vanguard' engine was fitted, developing 68 bhp at 4,250 rev/min, the model being called the '2000'.

Features: A very distinctive car of unique body styling. Strong chassis and aluminium bodywork ideal features for successful restoration (front wings must be maintained against corrosion). Spares still fairly readily available (see sources below). Low compression ratio enables cheaper low-octane fuel to be used. Twin SUs may be fitted on 'TR2' manifold to increase performance of 'Roadster 2000'.

Failings: Ash body frame must be thoroughly inspected for rot and sections replaced. Unequal weight displacement causes skidding at low speeds on greasy surfaces.

1948 Triumph '1800' Roadster

Triumph 'TR2'

1953-55. 2-litre Sports. 2 seater

At the 1952 Motor Show, Triumph displayed their prototype of a new series, a sports car called the 'TR1'. It had been built up from a variety of Standard-Triumph parts — the chassis was adapted from that of the old Standard 'Ten', the axles and suspension were taken from their 'knife-edge' saloon, the Triumph 'Mayflower', while the engine and gearbox unit was a modified version of that used in the Standard 'Vanguard'. Body design was by W.J. Belgrove and the design team was led by Harry Webster. The production model, the 'TR 2', emerged in 1953 priced at £965; its tremendous success, together with that of the later 'TR 3', helped Triumph over a financial crisis. The 'TR 2' was distinctive with its radiator situated behind a ducted air-intake and the front wings blended into the bonnet moulding, together with the headlamps. The line of the front wings extended rearwards to butt-joint against the rear wings (as in the Jaguar 'XK 120' and the Jowett 'Jupiter' of that era). The hotted-up 'Vanguard'-based engine was of 1,991cc, delivering 91 bhp at 4,880 rev/min. The compression ratio was high at 8.5 to 1. Top speed was 105 mile/h. The brakes were fully hydraulic; suspension was by coil springs on the front wheels and leaf springs on the rear. A four-speed 'floor-change' gearbox was fitted.

Features: Compact enough for a thorough restoration. Engine spares quite readily obtained. True chassis incorporated. Orthodox engine design. Thousands of enthusiast owners.

1954 Triumph 'TR2'
(*Copyright of the TR Register*)

1954 Triumph 'TR2'
(*Copyright of the TR Register*)

Failings: Many 'TR's are 'thrashed' before re-sale (beware). Steel bodywork will need constant maintenance. Rather noisy engine.

Car Club Honorary Secretary: No official club recognised by the RAC.
('TR Register':) T. Simpson, 100, High St, Redbourne, St. Albans, Herts.
(Triumph 'Roadster' Club:) **R.A. Fitsall, 80 Link Lane, Wallington, Surrey.**

SPARES: 1. Standard-Triumph stockists, to a degree.
2. A.T. Johnson, Paradise Road, Downham Market, Norfolk.
3. Crawley 23477.
4. (Hoods:) Mitchell, Iden Court, Frittenden Road, Staplehurst, Kent or, London Trimming Co. Ltd., Store F, Marshgate Estate, Taplow, Nr. Maidenhead, Berks.
5. ('TR 2' fibreglass wings and sills:) P.M.A. Accessories Ltd., 30-31, Tudor Chambers, Station Rd, Wood Green, London N.22.
6. ('Roadster' spares:) A. Harold, Villa Dumka, 39 Fairfax Rd, Teddington, Middx. (01-977 1730)
7. (Wiring looms — new) R. & T. Daly (Auto Electricians), 8 Becontree Avenue, Dagenham, Essex (01-599 1772).
8. Through above clubs.

	Triumph '1800' Roadster	'2000' Roadster*	Triumph 'TR2'
Engine (Mechanical)			
No. of cylinders : capacity	4; 1,776 cc	4; 2088 cc	4; 1,991 cc
Bore and stroke	73 x 106 mm	85 x 92 mm	83 x 92 mm
Compression ratio	6·72 : 1	6·7 : 1	8·5 : 1
Valve layout	Overhead		Overhead
Tappet clearances	Inlet 0·012 in.		Inlet 0·010 in.
	Exhaust 0·012 in.		Exhaust 0·012 in.
Location of valve timing marks	On timing gears		On timing gears
Timing : inlet valve opens	10° btdc		15° btdc (normal)
Piston withdrawal direction	Downwards	Upwards	Downwards

	Triumph '1800' Roadster	'2000' Roadster*	Triumph 'TR2'
Engine (Ignition)			
Firing order	1, 3, 4, 2		1, 3, 4, 2
Location of timing marks	On crankshaft pulley and timing cover		On crankshaft pulley and timing cover
Timing : points open	tdc		4° btdc
Original spark plugs	Champion LIOS		Champion LIOS
Plug gap	0·025 in.		0·032 in.
Original (Lucas) coil	B12		B12
Original (Lucas) distributor	DKYH4A		DM2
Carburettors			
Original make	Solex	Solex	2 SU
Original type	35FAIE	32BIO	H6
Choke tube	25	25	Metering Needle SM
Main jet	125	135	—
Compensating jet	250	190	—
Pilot jet	50	55	—
Air bleed	1·5	—	—
Starter jet	125	130	—
Electrical Accessories			
Battery	12v 63 ah		12v 51 ah
Original (Lucas) generator	C45YV	C39PV	C39PV/2LO
Original (Lucas) control box	RF91	RF95	RB106/1
Original (Lucas) starter motor	M418G-O	M418G	M418G
Chassis Components and Steering Geometry			
Brakes	Girling hydrastatic		Lockheed hydraulic
Rear axle : Type	Spiral bevel	Hypoid	Hypoid bevel
Ratio	4·57 : 1	4·625 : 1	3·7 : 1
Crown-wheel tooth contact	Adjustable	Not adjustable	Adjustable
Front suspension	Transverse semi-elliptic leaf		Lateral coil
Rear suspension	Semi-elliptic leaf		Semi-elliptic leaf
Steering pattern	Cam and double roller		Bishop cam and lever
Toe-in	Nil		$1/8$ in
Castor angle	6°		Nil
Camber angle	1¾°		2°
King-pin inclination	8½°		7°
Lubrication			
Engine : Original S.A.E. grade	Summer 30, Winter 20		Summer 30, Winter 20
Quantity	14 pt.	12 pt.	12 pt. from dry
Gearbox : Original S.A.E. grade	30	90 HYP	30
Quantity	2 pt.	1½ pt.	1½ pt. (overdrive 3½ pt.)
Rear axle : Original S.A.E. grade	140 EP	90 HYP	90 HYP
Quantity	2¾ pt.	2 pt.	1½ pt.
Steering box : Original S.A.E. grade	140 EP		90 EP
Tyres			
Size	5·75–6·00 x 16		5·50 x 15
Pressures (lb/in^2)	F : 22 R : 24		F : 22 R : 24

Note: Details of the '2000' are identical with the '1800' except where stated in the second column.

Wolseley '4/50'

1948-52. 1½-litre Saloon. 5 seater

The Wolseley Company was purchased by Morris Motors in 1927, hence all subsequent designs reflected this factor. The '4/50' (four cylinders, 50 bhp) of 1948 resembled very closely the Morris body designs of the same era, in fact the larger '6/80' had a contemporary Morris 'Six' body with a Wolseley radiator grille substituted. Powering the '4/50' was an ohc engine of 1,475cc capacity and 6.5 to 1 compression ratio, delivering, as stated above, 50 bhp at 4,500 rev/min. Top speed was 70 mile/h and fuel consumption 30-32 mpg. This basic design of ohc engine gave an excellent all round performance, the larger six-cylinder engined '6/80' of 2,214cc being adopted by the Metropolitan Police Force during its production years. The bodywork of the '4/50' was of pressed steel and of monocoque unit-construction; fully hydraulic brakes were fitted and the suspension was independent on the front

1948 Wolseley '4/50'

wheels by torsion bars, with leaf-springs on the rear. Traditionally British interior appointments were included, with upholstery in leather and a veneered dashboard. The steering column was of adjustable telescopic type, and a column-mounted gear lever operated the four-speed gearbox.

Features: Ohc engine gives lively performance; completely orthodox in design. Realistic fuel consumption. Torsion bar front suspension. Fully hydraulic brakes. Very comfortable, well-appointed interior.

Failings: Steel bodywork, and unit sub-frame very prone to corrosion. Engine and body spares scarce. Column gear-change not as positive as central lever would have been.

Wolseley '6/90'

1954-56. 2½-litre Saloon. 5 seater

Following the '4/50' and '6/80' models came more 'modern' designs, the '4/44' of 1952 and '6/90' of 1954. In fact, the body design of the '6/90' was virtually identical to that of the Riley 'Pathfinder' of 1953, a Wolseley radiator grille being substituted together with other small fittings to make the transformation more effective. This new Wolseley model gave the impression of a 'scaled-up 4/44' with its bulky bonnet and wings and large side-area, all trace of the prewar squareness of line having finally vanished. A 2,639cc pushrod overhead-valve engine of 7.3 to 1 compression ratio was fitted, carburation being by twin SUs (as in the earlier '6/80') and the unit developed 90 bhp at 4,600 rev/min, giving a top speed of 90 mile/h. This was the same powerplant as used in the contemporary Austin A.90 'Westminster'. Bodywork of the '6/90' was of pressed steel, and the chassis of box-section components welded into a frame. Brakes were fully hydraulic and its suspension employed torsion bars on the front wheels, while the rear wheels were served by coil springs and radius arms. Steering pattern was Bishop cam as in the '4/50' and '6/80'.

Features: A large, smooth-running, comfortable car of sensible, unpretentious design. Completely orthodox BMC engine and chassis fittings, making overhaul very straightforward. Twin carburetters give quite lively performance. Excellent interior finish.

Failings: Steel chassis and bodywork — inevitable corrosion unless checked. Rather high fuel consumption.

Car Club Honorary Secretary: No club in existence for post-1948 Wolseley cars.

SPARES: Not very easy to find; British Leyland probably offer very few spares now. But parts from the engine of a 1954-56 Austin 'Westminster' could be transplanted into the '6/90'.

	Wolseley '4/50'	Wolseley '6/90'
Engine (Mechanical)		
No. of cylinders : capacity	4; 1,476 cc	6; 2,639 cc
Bore and stroke	73·5 x 87 mm	79·4 x 88·9 mm
Compression ratio	7 : 1	7·3 : 1
Valve layout	overhead (ohc)	overhead (pushrod)
Tappet clearances	0·015 in (hot)	0·012 in. (hot)
Location of valve timing marks	On flywheel and camshaft bearing	On timing wheels and bright chain links
Timing : inlet valve opens	8° btdc	5° btdc
Piston withdrawal direction	Upwards	Upwards
Engine (Ignition)		
Firing order	1, 3, 4, 2	1, 5, 3, 6, 2, 4
Location of timing marks	On flywheel	On timing cover and pulley
Timing : points open	tdc, fully retarded	6° btdc
Original spark plugs	Champion L-10	Champion N8B
Plug gap	0·020 in.	0·022 in.
Original (Lucas) coil	Q12	HA12
Original (Lucas) distributor	DVXH4A	DM6
Carburetters		
Original make	SU	2 SU
Original type	H2	H4
Choke tube	—	1½ in.
Metering Needle	EM	GR
Electrical Accessories		
Battery	12v 51 ah	12v 51 ah
Original (Lucas) generator	C39PV/2	C45PV/5
Original (Lucas) control box	RB106/1	RB106/2
Original (Lucas) starter motor	M35G/1	M418G
Chassis Components and Steering Geometry		
Brakes	Lockheed hydraulic	Lockheed hydraulic
Rear axle : Type	Hypoid bevel	Hypoid bevel
Ratio	4·55 or 4·875 : 1	4·1 : 1
Crown-wheel tooth contact	Adjustable by spacers	Adjustable by spacers and shims
Front suspension	Torsion bars	Torsion bars
Rear suspension	Semi-elliptic leaf	Coil springs and radius arms
Steering Pattern	Bishop cam	Bishop cam
Toe-in	Nil	Nil
Castor angle	3°	3°
Camber angle	0–½° positive	1°
King-pin inclination	9°	6°
Lubrication		
Engine : Original S.A.E. grade	30	30
Quantity	7 pt.	11½ pt.
Gearbox : Original S.A.E. grade	90	30
Quantity	1¾ pt.	4½ pt.
Rear axle : Original S.A.E. grade	90 HYP	90 HYP
Quantity	1¾ pt.	3¾ pt.
Steering box : Original S.A.E. grade	90 EP	90 HYP
Tyres		
Size	5·50 x 15	6·00 x 15
Pressures (lb/in^2)	F : 26 R : 28	F : 28 R : 28

1954 Wolseley '6/90'

Appendix I
Spark Plug Data

Original plug	Modern equivalent	Alternative modern equivalents			
CHAMPION		AC	Autolite	KLG	Lodge
C7	7	C85 or 85H	—	—	C3
L7	L7	44F	—	F70	H 14
L10	L10	45F	—	F50	CN
L10S	L7	44F	—	F70	H14
N8	N8	46N or 46XL	AG5	FE50	CLNH
N8B	N8	46N or 46 XL	AG5	FE50	CLNH
NA8	N5	45XL	AG3	FE70	HBLN
NA10	N3	43XL	—	FE100	2HLN
KLG		AC	Autolite	Champion	Lodge
L50					
P10					
P10L					
PT.L70	T90	—	PE3	Z10	2HL10
PT.L80					
10L30					
LODGE		AC	Autolite	Champion	KLG
CB14	CLNH	46XL or 46N	AG5	N8	FE50
CLNH	CLNH	46XL or 46N	AG5	N8	FL50
H14	H14	44F	—	L7	F70
HLN	HLN	—	AG2	N4	FE80
HLNP	HBLN	45XL	AG3	N5	FE70
HLNR	CLNH	46XL or 46N	AG5	N8	FE50
HN	HN	—	AE4	L85	F80
HNP	HN	—	AE4	L85	F80

Appendix II
Sources of Spares and Materials, Special Services, Specialist Manufacturers

ALLOY WELDING

Liselott Welding Service, 9a Broadway, Bexleyheath, Kent.
(cylinder heads, crankcases)

BEARINGS

Motor Imports, 17A Seeley Rd, London SW 17. (ball- and roller-bearings)

BRAKE AND SPEEDOMETER CABLES

Speedy Cables, 10-12 Gaskin St, London N1. (made up to pattern, any type)
Thomas Richfield & Son, Ltd, 8, Broadstone Place, Baker Street, London W.1.
(speedo, tachometer and clock repairs also)

BRAKE LININGS

Listers', 93 Carlisle Rd, Bradford 8, Yorks. (any pair re-lined, £1.25 inc. post)
Motolympia, Welshpool, Montgomeryshire. (Welshpool 2327.)

BRAKE MECHANISMS

Ferodo Ltd, Chapel-en-le-Frith, Stockport, Cheshire.
Girling Ltd, Kings Rd, Tyseley, Birmingham 11.
Lockheed Hydraulic Brake Co. Ltd, Leamington Spa, Warwicks.
Patent Enterprises, Ltd, 143-145 Kew Rd, Richmond, Surrey. ('ABV' automatic
brake-bleed valves — no assistant needed)

CARBURETTERS

Anglo-American Electrical and Carburetter Services Ltd, 134-138 Norwood Rd,
London SE 24. (postal service)
BGE, 16 Wakering Rd, Barking, Essex. (Solex, Stromberg, Zenith)
Deeprose SUper Centre, Station Garage, Burnt Ash Hill, London S.E.12 OHN. (SU
carburetters, postal service)
SU Carburetter Co. Ltd, Wood Lane, Erdington, Birmingham 24.
Zenith Carburetter Co. Ltd., Honey Pot Lane, Stanmore, Middx. (Solex, Stromberg
also)

ELECTRICAL INSTRUMENTS AND EQUIPMENT

Kenlowe Accessories & Co. Ltd, Burchetts Green, Maidenhead, Berks. (Littlewick
Green 3303.) ('Kenlowe' electric radiator fan)
Joseph Lucas Ltd, Great King Street, Birmingham 19.

FIBREGLASS MATERIALS IN BULK

Glasplies, 68 Park Rd, Southport, Lancs.
Solent Plastics, 30 Mary Street, Birmingham 3. (021-744 7944)
Strand Glass Co. Ltd, (1) 109 High Street, Brentford, Middx. (2) 980 Stockport
Rd, Manchester 10. (3) 72 London Rd, Southampton.

GASKETS

Lipscombe & Hessey, Victoria Rd, Eton Wick, Windsor, Berks. (Windsor 64413.)
(cylinder head and manifold gaskets hand-made to pattern)

GEARBOX SPARES

Motolympia, Welshpool, Montgomeryshire. (Welshpool 2327.) (Spares for
1930-1965)

GEARBOX REPAIRS

North London Transmission Services, 80 Markhouse Rd, Walthamstow, London
E.17. (01-520 5800) (any type, postal service also)

GENERAL SPARES

Autobreakers, 40 North Street, Old Isleworth, Middx. (01-560 8062, no postal)
Motolympia, Welshpool, Montgomeryshire. (Welshpool 2327.) (1930 onwards)
Padgets', Welney, Nr. Wisbech, Lincs. (Welney 225.) (1918-1955 spares)
41, High Street, West Lavington, Devizes, Wilts. (spares for 1920-1950)

HOME CHROMIUM PLATING *(No electricity needed)*

Dominion Distributors, 93 Judd Street, London WC1H 9NG.
Klensyl Products, 56 Norman Rd, Sutton, Surrey. (postal service)

HOME GANTRY AND HOIST, FOR ENGINE LIFTING

Gantry and Hoist (mnfg.) Co, 52 Bell Green, Sydenham, London SE26 £8.82)

HOODS

The Car Hood Co., Southern House, 73 Southern Row, Ladbroke Grove, London
W 10. (01-969 7148)
Don Trimming Co. Ltd, 2A Hampton Rd, Erdington, Birmingham, B23 7JJ.
(021-373 1313)

INTERIOR TRIMMING MATERIALS

The Car Hood Co., Southern House, 73 Southern Row, Ladbroke Grove, London
W 10. (01-969 7148)
Edgware Motor Accessories, 120 High Street, Edgware, Middx. (Edgware 4789.)

NICKEL PLATING
The Complete Automobilist Ltd., 39 Main Street, Baston, Peterborough. (Greatford 312.) (quick service)

PISTONS, RINGS, CYLINDER LINERS, ETC
Hepworth & Grandage Ltd, St. John's Works, Bradford 4. ('Hepolite' products)

RADIATORS
Raymond Radiators Ltd.   (1) 60 Chalk Farm Rd, London NW 1. (01-485 6195).
(2) 5 Ware Rd, Hertford, Herts. (Hertford 4012)
73 Trafalgar Avenue, Peckham, London SE 15. (repairs and replacements)

SHOCKABSORBERS
J.W.E. Banks & Sons Ltd., Crowland, Peterborough, PE6 0JP, (Crowland 316) ('Koni' products)
Clares Motor Works Ltd, 260 Knights Hill, London SE 27.
Janspeed Engineering Ltd., Southampton Rd, Salisbury, Wilts. (Salisbury 22002/22181) ('Armstrong' appointed stockists)
Young's, 18-37 Tooting Bec Rd, London SW 17.

SPARK PLUGS
Champion Sparking Plug Co. Ltd., Great South West Rd, Feltham, Middx.

STRIPPED THREAD REPAIRS
Alf Snell, 126 Boundary Rd, London E. 17 (01-520 5222) (Spark plug holes, stripped studs, etc.)

SUSPENSION SPRINGS
Carsprings Ltd, Jute Lane, Brimsdown, Enfield, Middx. (01-804 5486.)

TYRES
Askew Tyres, 138 Askew Rd, Shepherds Bush, London W 12. (large rims, £6.00)
The Dunlop Tyre Co. Ltd, Fort Dunlop, Erdington, Birmingham 24.
E.H. Hamilton & Son, 22-24 Vicarage Street, Yeovil, Somerset. (Yeovil 3927.) (veteran and vintage)
Hampstead Tyres, 31 Fortune Green Rd, London NW 6. (01-435 8988.)
Pentonville Tyre Service, 1 Penton Street, Pentonville Rd, London N 1. (16, 17, 18in. rims)
Vintage Tyre Supplies, Jackman Mews, North Circular Rd, Neasdon, London NW NW 10. (01-450 6468.)

WIRING HARNESSES
Autosparks Ltd. Lime St, Hull, Yorks. HU8 7AH. (0482-20719) (Brand new, all cars from 1932)

VALVES AND GUIDES

John Bland, 27 Southfields Rd, London SW 18. (01-874 1612) (valves and guides made up to pattern)

MODERN EQUIVALENTS FOR LUCAS ACCESSORIES

Service Information Department, Light Vehicle Section, Joseph Lucas (Sales and Service) Ltd., Great Hampton Street, Birmingham B18 6AU.

Index